Finding Freedom From Worry and Stress

women of faith™

FINDING FREEDOM FROM WORRY AND STRESS

BY

CHRISTA KINDE

FOREWORD BY

THELMA WELLS

THOMAS NELSON
Since 1798

© 2003 Thomas Nelson.

Previously published as *Living Above Worry and Stress*.

The publishers are grateful to Christa Kinde for her collaboration, writing skills, and editorial help in developing the content for this book.

Published in Nashville, Tennessee, by Thomas Nelson. Thomas Nelson is a registered trademark of HarperCollins Christian Publishing, Inc.

Thomas Nelson titles may be purchased in bulk for educational, business, fund-raising, or sales promotional use. For information, please e-mail SpecialMarkets@ ThomasNelson.com.

Scripture taken from The Holy Bible, New King James Version (NKJV). © 1979, 1980, 1982 by Thomas Nelson. Used by permission. All rights reserved.

Scripture quotations marked NCV are taken from The Holy Bible: New Century Version, (NCV). © 1987, 1988, 1991 by Thomas Nelson. Used by permission. All rights reserved.

Scripture quotations marked NLT are taken from The Holy Bible, New Living Translation (NLT). © 1986 by the Tyndale House Publishers, Wheaton, Illinois, 60189. Used by permission. All rights reserved.

ISBN: 978-0-3106-8-2554

First Printing February 2016/Printed in the United States of America

⫸ CONTENTS ⫷

Foreword

According to a Gallup poll, most women are concerned about time, family, health, and money. Wouldn't you know it? All the things that cause us to worry and fret have to do with stuff God has given us dominion over.

We have one hundred and sixty-eight hours per week to do whatever we NEED to do. But oh no, we spend much of that precious time worrying about how much time we don't have.

God has instinctively given us the common sense and the innate ability to have a wholesome relationship with our family. We try to discipline the young ones, only to be afraid of damaging their ego. We attempt to control the grown ones, only to discover that we overstress ourselves because they are old enough to make their own decisions and we can't stop them.

Our bodies tell us what's going on but we don't listen. If we do listen we don't do anything about it. Oh no, we are too busy doing everything else but eating right, exercising, and getting the rest we need.

And money, well, it doesn't matter how much we get, we still want more. We use credit cards that must be paid every month to spend money we don't have to buy things we don't want to impress people we don't like.

What's wrong with this picture? It seems that women just have to have something to worry and be stressed about. Really! We don't have to be this way! We can actually live above worry and stress. (That's unproductive stress, of course.) The kind of stress that causes us to have headaches, backaches, shingles, upset stomachs, strokes, and heart attacks.

I should know! Now, I don't mean I never contemplate worrying and becoming stressful. I've just found the path to overcoming the temptation of worrying and being stressful. This knowledge has come about because of the sleepless nights I've had. The years of poor health and mental depression I suffered. The wasted hours of self-pity and defaming self-talk I inflicted on myself. The grasp for things, things, and more things I thought I needed. The broken relationships that I tried to fix that were really none of my business. And the fear that I was not going to be successful in all these areas.

This informative, instructional, encouraging, empowering, influential book addresses many of the issues in a woman's life that causes her to worry and be stressful. Come with us and discover the practical ways you can eliminate the negative of worry and stress. Study the scriptures that will give you strength and courage to face the issues in your life. Listen to the stories to see how the writers handle situations similar to yours. Begin immediately to apply and practice the principles in the probing. You'll see yourself, day by day, little by little laying aside the weight of worry and stress that can easily wear you down, and beginning to stand tall with a light heart of faith and trust in God. He will monitor your thoughts and disable your mind of worry and stress. After all, John 16:33 declares that, "In this world you will have trouble. But be of good cheer. God has overcome the world."

—*Thelma Wells*

⚔ Introduction ⚔

Consider the lilies, how they grow: they neither toil nor spin; and yet I say to you, even Solomon in all his glory was not arrayed like one of these. If then God so clothes the grass, which today is in the field and tomorrow is thrown into the oven, how much more will He clothe you, O you of little faith.

Luke 12:27–28, NKJV

The words echo back to us from years gone by. We first learned it in a Vacation Bible School one summer or from a dear Sunday school teacher—the voice of Jesus calling us to consider the lilies. The lesson was a simple one: don't worry. If God would give the flowers such pretty petals, dressing them more grandly than wealthy King Solomon could manage, He will provide for our needs, too.

Unfortunately, the call to consider the lilies is left on a dusty shelf somewhere. It's probably right next to the old plea to stop and smell the roses. We're too busy for stopping. We're too rushed for consideration. Our "to do" lists are long. Our calendars are booked. Our time is money. We can't keep up.

We are busy people. We have responsibilities at work. We have responsibilities at home. We have responsibilities at church. We have responsibilities at school. We have responsibilities within our communities. We care for the needs of our parents, our husbands, our children, our siblings, our employers, our closest friends. Most days, it is more than we can handle. Our hearts are overwhelmed. We are stressed out. We are worried. We dread tomorrow.

In the midst of all this everyday turmoil, our hearts long for a place of peace. We know God has promised us rest. We know He says we don't have to worry about tomorrow. He promised to calm our fears. Yet we barely have time to whisper a prayer, let alone study our Bibles. If you have been struggling, come. Let's take a little time to explore the Scriptures, and find some practical guidelines for laying aside our fears, our worry, and even our stress. You really can discover a place of peace.

"From the end of the earth I will cry to You,
When my heart is overwhelmed;
Lead me to the rock that is higher than I."

Psalm 61:2, NKJV

CHAPTER ONE

SCATTERED LIVES

"A PRAYER OF ONE OVERWHELMED WITH TROUBLE, POURING OUT PROBLEMS BEFORE THE LORD. LORD, HEAR MY PRAYER! LISTEN TO MY PLEA! DON'T TURN AWAY FROM ME IN MY TIME OF DISTRESS. BEND DOWN YOUR EAR AND ANSWER ME QUICKLY WHEN I CALL TO YOU, FOR MY DAYS DISAPPEAR LIKE SMOKE."

Psalm 102:1–3, NLT

Sometimes we don't realize how busy we really are. Because we're right in the middle of living our lives, it feels quite normal. Sure, we don't get everything done that we *wanted* to, but then only Betty Crocker can do that! We'd like to slow down the hectic pace of our days a little, but there's just a lot going on right now.

Usually, my life doesn't feel *too* busy. However, nothing brings me up short like a visit back to my folks' home. They still live in the old brick farmhouse where I grew up. It's situated on ten acres, near a quaint little Scandinavian town. Whenever I go back for a visit, I'm amazed at how quietly they live.

They have to drive to the next town to do any real power shopping. The closest fast food restaurant is twenty minutes away. So is the nearest freeway. Usually, though, they just stay home. Dad keeps a vegetable garden, and Mom has a

CLEARING ↗ THE ↖ COBWEBS

When life gets busy, what's your favorite way to slow down — do the crossword puzzle in the paper, enjoy a long soak in the tub, stroll through the park, bum around the mall, page through a magazine, putter in the garden, go to bed early? How do you unwind and relax?

1

rose garden. They eat their own fruit and vegetables in season, and can the rest. Dad put up bluebird houses, and they watch the collections of birds that visit their feeders. One year, the biggest event during our visit came the night after a violent thunderstorm. Everyone piled into their car and drove around town, inspecting downed trees.

The pace of their life is steady. Their home is a quiet haven from a busy world. After I visit there, I return to my own home with the determination of creating my own haven. Although we don't all desire to live out in the country, we all want our homes to be a quiet place where people will want to linger.

I'm usually running behind, playing catch up, and robbing Petula to pay Paulette. Yet give me a day off, and it slips through my fingers (like my last paycheck). Then, the harder I try to hang on to special moments, the faster the clock seems to tick. Which ticks me off because the hard days, the painful days, the boring days, seem to contain endless hours.

Patsy Clairmont

1. What are your responsibilities around your home? You know, the things you absolutely have to do to stay afloat and can't delegate to anyone else in the family?

2. What are the occasional, maintenance-type tasks you have to make sure get done?

3. What activities do you attend on a regular basis, or act as chauffeur on your children's behalf?

4. What responsibilities do you hold in your church? How much preparation time do these responsibilities take?

I'll never forget the year I realized that I wasn't a kid anymore. I was twenty-four years old, but unfortunately it still came as a bit of a shock. Christmas had arrived, and my husband and I put up the tree and decorated our little apartment. The cookies were baked, the stockings were hung, and the Christmas cards had been mailed. This was going to be a special year, for it was the first holiday for our eight-month old daughter.

Boxes started to arrive from back home, and anticipation began to build as we stacked them next to the tree. Part of our tradition was to not open the boxes as they arrived, even though we knew they were filled with smaller packages. The temptation to rattle the smaller boxes was too great. We always waited until Christmas morning. By the time Christmas Eve had arrived, we were giddy with anticipation, for the stack of out-of-town packages was as tall as I was.

> *Have you ever raced so fast through the day that you find yourself wondering if there really is "the sweet by-and-by" out there someplace instead of the "toils and snares" of the moment? Sometimes the concept of rest and peace seems like nothing more than a luxurious figment of the imagination.*
>
> Luci Swindoll

When the morning arrived, I bounced my husband out of bed, declaring with a twinkle in my eye that it was Christmas, and Santa had come. We tore into the boxes together, and lifted out the brightly-colored boxes with their ribbons and bows. Every gift in the first big box was for our daughter. Hmmmmm. On to the next box. Again, everything was for our little girl. How could this be? She wasn't even old enough to care yet. Suddenly it dawned on me. I wasn't the little girl anymore, she was. Christmas wasn't going to be for me anymore, it was for her.

The next year I was ready for it. I bravely took up the mantle that had been my mother's before me. It was my turn to make the holidays happen for my family. Christmas traditions and memories were my responsibility now. I became the planner, the giver, the merry-maker.

5. Birthdays and holidays take a lot of planning. These annual events are traditions, and you are the keeper of the traditions. What seasonal celebrations do you make "happen" for your family?

> *Scripture is filled with encouragement for our faith because we are so vulnerable to doubt and fear when we feel overwhelmed by life.*
>
> Barbara Johnson

6. On top of all of these things, many of us have also taken on a job. Some of us are self-employed while others are working outside the home. How many hours do you work each week? Also, is it a job that you can leave at work, or do you find that your responsibilities weigh on your mind even while at home?

7. In the midst of all this busyness and business, what would you say are the most important things in your life?

8. Look at these last few pages. Here are lists of all the people you are responsible for and all the jobs you must do. Do you feel overwhelmed by all these responsibilities? Do you have any fears or worries that crop up because of them?

9. Look at David's prayer in Psalm 102:1–3. How is he feeling?

10. We know from the Bible that "God is not the author of confusion" (1 Cor. 14:33, NKJV). Fear, worry, and stress are not a part of His plan for our lives. When He made you, what did He have in mind for His workmanship? Look in Ephesians 2:10.

> *I don't know about you, but I'm susceptible to viewing the lives of others from afar and believing their existence is easier, calmer, and more meaningful than mine—rather paradisiacal. Not all the time, mind you, but I do have those moments when I give way to envy because I'm trudging through a dreary season while someone else seems to be skipping down a well-lit path.*
>
> Patsy Clairmont

DIGGING DEEPER

Though our busyness overwhelms us at times, we are never admonished to embrace the other extreme. The Proverbs are filled with scathing criticisms of lazy people. Slothfulness is considered so awful, it is one of the infamous seven deadly sins! Somewhere, there's a balance between busyness and laziness. Let's explore a few Scriptures that encourage us to remain industrious women.

- Proverbs 6:6–8
- Proverbs 12:24
- Proverbs 13:4
- Proverbs 31:10–31
- Colossians 3:23
- 2 Timothy 2:15

PONDER & PRAY

Are you feeling busy? Is the busyness too much to handle? As you pray this week, follow David's example and cry out to the Lord. Pour out your heart before Him, and tell Him about the strain you are under. Ask God to help you see what is important to *Him* in your days. Then ask God to guide you in organizing your time. His leading and inspiration will turn you to the path He has prepared for you.

TRINKETS TO TREASURE

At the close of each lesson, you will be presented with a small gift. Though imaginary, it will serve to remind you of the things you have learned. Think of it as a souvenir! Souvenirs are little trinkets we pick up on our journeys to remind us of where we have been. They keep us from forgetting the path we have traveled. Hide these little treasures in your heart, for as you ponder on them, they will draw you closer to God!

When our lives get too hectic, we start to feel as scattered as the leaves we see in autumn. At first, they are lovely, but then they begin to fall. The leaves become a clutter on the lawn. Every gust of wind brings a new torrent of disarray, and no matter how furiously we rake, we can't bring those scattered leaves together again. Your trinket for the week is a leaf. Let it serve to remind you of how scattered your days can feel. Make it your prayer that your life will not remain a tumult of dried leaves, drifting around with every breath of wind. Ask instead that your life might be as fresh as a newly unfurled leaf, clinging to the strength and stability of the tree branch. This study guide may be your chance to "turn over a new leaf!"

NOTES & PRAYER REQUESTS

CHAPTER TWO

FEAR AND TREMBLING

"WHENEVER I AM AFRAID, I WILL TRUST IN YOU."

Psalm 56:3, NKJV

When I was a child, I had my little fears. When day was done, I needed certain reassurances at bedtime. One was my teddy bear, ingeniously named Teddy. She was my constant companion. Then there was my nightlight. I could see its orange glow from my bed, and it comforted me when the nights seemed too dark.

Many of us now struggle with very grown-up fears. Are you afraid of rejection? Are you afraid your husband is being unfaithful? Are you afraid you might lose your job? Are you afraid your son is doing drugs? Are you afraid your daughter is getting in with the wrong crowd? Are you afraid the diagnosis will be cancer? Are you afraid your parents will never become Christians? Are you afraid of divorce? Are you afraid of bad men—thieves, kidnappers, murderers, rapists, and terrorists? Are you afraid of loneliness? Are you afraid of growing old? Are you afraid of saying the wrong thing? Are you afraid God doesn't really love you anymore? Are you still afraid of the dark?

CLEARING ⚓ THE ⚓ COBWEBS

Did you ever have a special blanket you always carried with you, or a special stuffed animal you wouldn't go to bed without? What was your most precious stuffed animal's name?

9

Did you know the children of Israel had nightlights? The entire nation was afraid of the dark. In ancient times, the oil lamps that lit homes were kept burning all night long. It was so important to keep that lamp burning that poor people would spend their money on oil first, even if there wasn't enough left to buy food! God knew His people needed certain reassurances. So when they were uprooted from their homes and forced to pitch their tents in barren landscapes each night, they were comforted by the presence of a pillar of fire. The glow it cast over the sleeping camp reminded the children of Israel their Constant Companion was near.

1. Were you ever afraid of the dark? Did you have bad dreams when you were little? What comfort does Psalm 91:5 and Proverbs 3:24 provide?

2. These days, just watching the evening news can leave us a bit uneasy. Planes crash, diseases spread, buildings burn, corporations crumble, and wars rage. When all the news seems to be bad news, what comfort can we find? Look at Psalm 112:7.

> *Fear is indiscriminate. It affects all of us regardless of our age or position in life. Whether our fear is absolutely realistic or out of proportion in our minds, our greatest refuge is Jesus Christ.*
>
> Luci Swindoll

3. God thinks of everything, and His promises can comfort our hearts. Gossip and rumors are vicious, and misunderstandings can injure a relationship. Some of us are afraid of what people might say about us, but what does Isaiah 51:7 promise?

4. Some of us are afraid of pain and death. Though we do not suffer from religious persecution as some of our sisters around the world do, we tremble at the prospect of another terrorist attack. What does Jesus tell His believers in Luke 12:4?

We tend to think of the men and women we find in the Bible as brave. Their reputations are filled with honor, courage, and faithfulness. However, if we take a quick look through the Scriptures, it isn't hard to discover people's fears.

Eve was afraid she was missing out on something (Gen. 3:5). Jacob was afraid his brother would take revenge upon him (Gen. 27:41–43). Moses was afraid to speak in public (Ex. 4:10). Aaron was afraid to take a stand and say no (Ex. 32:4). David was afraid

> *Sometimes we are afraid to reach out and live the life that we believe we have been called to. But fear is no friend. It may seem to protect, but it slowly suffocates.*
>
> Sheila Walsh

his sin would be discovered (2 Sam. 11:15). Solomon was afraid he would make a bad leader (1 Kin. 3:9). Jonah was afraid to face the enemy of his people (Jon. 1:3). Esther was afraid of admitting her family background (Esth. 2:10). Hezekiah was afraid of dying (2 Kin. 20:1–3). Joseph was afraid of what people would say (Matt. 1:19). The disciples were afraid of asking dumb questions (Mark 9:32). Jairus was afraid his child would die (Luke 8:41–42). Martha was afraid of disappointing her guests (Luke 10:40). Paul was afraid people wouldn't believe him (Acts 9:26). Felix was afraid to face the truth of the gospel (Acts 24:25). Peter was afraid of breaking traditions (Gal. 2:14).

God often calls us to take courage, even in the face of plaguing fears, and do what we know we should. The ultimate honor is given to the man or woman who fears God above all else.

5. In the face of little qualms, emotional mayhem, and our worst fears, Jesus has one thing to say to us. Turn to Mark 5:36. What does our Lord urge us to do?

6. So, we are not supposed to be afraid. Why? Matthew 10:31 offers a very good reason. What is it?

7. Let's consider Isaiah 12:2. What declarations and promises in the verse would dispel your fears?

8. Marilyn Meberg says, "For me to fear the unseen and worry about its potential to do harm throttles my joy." Still, the fact remains that we do have fearful moments. What do we need to remind ourselves *whenever* fears creep in? Psalm 56:3 holds the formula.

There resides in the heart of every believer little pockets of fear. For some of us it's cowardice. For others, it's timidity. Although we know the Savior gives courage and power, sometimes we feel safer in our little pocket than in His big provision. So we cower inside, afraid to be bold. We permit our human frailty to stand in the way of His strength.

Luci Swindoll

9. One last word of encouragement for the faint of heart. Trust God and His plans. No matter what might happen on this earth, what does God have in store for you in the end?

Digging Deeper

So many passages in the Bible are an encouragement to those whose hearts tremble. Let's explore some of the passages that encourage us to leave our fears behind.

- Genesis 15:1
- Deuteronomy 31:8
- Psalm 27:1
- Isaiah 41:10
- John 14:27

Ponder & Pray

When we find ourselves hindered by our fears, we are in good company. Many of the men and women in the Bible had to be calmed by the words "Fear not." Lay out your secret dread before your loving Lord. He already knows what you hide in your heart, and He longs to take away your fears. Pray this week that God will give you the grace to trust Him, no matter what turns your life may take.

Trinkets to Treasure

When night begins to fall, our fears seem to gain strength, and so your little gift this week is a nightlight. A nightlight is a promise of sweet sleep! It will remind you that you don't need to be afraid of the dark—or anything. If a troubled heart wakens you in the night, turn your eyes toward the light and whisper the words of the Psalmist, "Whenever I am afraid, I will trust in You." You are precious to God, and He will take care of you. Trust Him to do just that.

NOTES & PRAYER REQUESTS

CHAPTER THREE

WORRY WARTS

**"GIVE ALL YOUR WORRIES AND CARES TO GOD,
FOR HE CARES ABOUT WHAT HAPPENS TO YOU."**

1 Peter 5:7, NKJV

*O*nce upon a time, when we lived in the country, my husband bought himself a dog. She was a mild-mannered creature—smart and generally obedient. Her mother had been a black lab, and her father had been a St. Bernard—she had silky black hair and *really* big feet. Though she had inherited her mother's good looks and her father's calm temperament, I dubbed the puppy "Calamity."

One day, this Calamity of a dog was taking her beauty rest in her crate—an indoor doggie kennel of sorts. My husband had crafted a lovely top for the crate, which we then placed close to the front door. It was handy for the dog and also made a great place to set car keys, mail, and the like. On this particular day, our family was going out, and since the weather was mild, we left our jackets behind. Unfortunately, my daughter tossed hers rather haphazardly onto the top of Calamity's crate. While we were away, that dog wiggled and pawed and licked at that coat until she managed to catch the corner. That was all she needed.

CLEARING ↗ THE ↖ COBWEBS

Have you ever forgotten somebody's birthday, or maybe an important anniversary? When did you realize the slip, and what happened next?

15

By the time we got home, the damage was done. Pink polar fleece littered the floor of Calamity's crate and the floor of the entryway. She had managed to remove several of the snaps from the jacket, and they were piled in one corner of her abode. My daughter dissolved into tears as the guilty-looking pet was put out on her chain. Yanking the jacket back through the bars of the crate, I held it up to the light. The huge holes and matted fabric were irreparable. It was time to shop for a new jacket.

Worry is a vividly descriptive word. We tend to equate it with fear and anxiety, but we mustn't miss the subtle differences here. When you think of the word worry, think of a dog chewing up a pink polar fleece jacket. You see, the dictionary definition of worry is "to seize with the teeth and shake or tug at repeatedly." The action of repeatedly pulling at, picking at, gnawing, chewing, and toying with something is worrying at it. When we go over and over our concerns in our minds, worrying them continually, there can be no peace.

> *Sometimes, despite our best intentions, we find ourselves wandering in a wilderness of anxiety, lost and unable to find our way out. I know. For years I felt that way. Nothing seemed to work; I felt stripped and anxious, unable to determine what my mission in life should be."*
>
> Thelma Wells

1. Is there a difference between fear and worry? There's a hint in Romans 8:38.

2. God doesn't want us to be fearful people. Neither does He want us to be worriers. The secret fears we harbor in our hearts give rise to the worries that plague our minds. What is the result of worry on a person? Solomon offers some words of wisdom in Proverbs 12:25.

3. Jesus knows our days have their cares. What are the everyday things you worry about?

> *When somebody calls me with bad news, or my kids call me with problems they're facing, I ask myself, "What does the Word say?" Don't worry about it. Be anxious for nothing. Why shouldn't we worry about it? Because worry says to God, "Lord, I don't trust You." But we do worry, and then what?*
>
> Thelma Wells

4. Our Savior knows about all our concerns, but He pleaded with His followers not to have "an anxious mind" (Luke 12:29, NKJV). In Matthew 6:25–34, Jesus says not to worry about tomorrow. Why not?

5. Sometimes it's hard not to peek ahead on our schedules and start to fuss about what will be going on later in the week. We know we shouldn't be worrying, but it comes so *naturally*! It's actually hard to face our days just one at a time. What worries would disappear for you if you concentrated on the day you are in?

> *Worry never empties tomorrow of its sorrow, but it does empty it of its strength. Don't let anyone rob you of your confidence in God. Know His Word. Hold on to His hand. He will make your impossible mission possible and your life so much more than bearable.*
>
> Barbara Johnson

17

y mother-in-law and I have affectionate nicknames for each other. I call her Mary and she calls me Martha. You may recall the story of Lazarus' two sisters in the city of Bethany (John 11:1). Jesus commended Mary for choosing that which was most important, while Martha was gently scolded by her Teacher for caring too much about supper preparations. "Martha, Martha, you are worried and troubled about so many things" (Luke 10:41, TEV). My Mary mother-in-law spends much of her time in prayer and resting in the Lord. I, on the other hand, find it difficult to be still and like to keep my hands busy. Though I am not a worrier by nature, and do not borrow trouble from the days ahead, I do tend to worry in the same way Martha did. I get caught up in the business of *this* day! So much to do, so many places to go, so many people to see. I'd encourage you to follow the Lord's advice, and don't worry about tomorrow, but remember not to worry over today either!

6. We have just one option when it comes to facing worry. Read Philippians 4:6. What does Paul say worriers should do?

> My times of silence before God are very important to me. When I'm quiet, life falls into perspective for me. I have a very active mind and I'm a worrier, but in those moments when I choose to put that away, I rest beside the Shepherd in still places.
>
> Sheila Walsh

7. Peter has the same idea Paul had about worry. Read 1 Peter 5:7. What are we told to do about our worries?

DIGGING DEEPER

Have you ever done a character study in the Bible? This is your chance. Read everything recorded about these two very different sisters, Mary and Martha. They were dear friends of Jesus, and He was often a guest in their home. What can you learn about their personalities from this snapshot of their lives? Read through Luke 10:38–42, chapter 11 of John's Gospel, and John 12:1–8. Record your insights.

PONDER & PRAY

Take a look around your heart and mind this week, and see if you find worries lurking where they do not belong. If you find more than you expected, start a list! When you find a concern that is plaguing your heart and occupying your mind, cast it away. Turn to the Lord who knows and loves you, and surrender that nagging burden through prayer. Once you relinquish it into His capable hands, you will discover peace.

TRINKETS TO TREASURE

Have you ever heard of a worry stone? Traditionally, it's a smooth, round rock you keep in your pocket. Whenever you start to feel worried about something, you slip your hand into your pocket and run your thumb over the surface. It's supposed to have a calming effect and release nervous tension. Well, your trinket this week is a worry stone, but I don't want you to carry it around with you. Place it on the windowsill near your sink, or on your bathroom counter. Whenever you see it, recall to mind that God can handle all your worries, and you can leave them with Him. Rather than carrying them with you, leave them at His feet.

Notes & Prayer Requests

_____

_____

_____

_____

_____

_____

_____

_____

_____

_____

_____

_____

_____

_____

_____

_____

_____

_____

_____

_____

_____

_____

_____

CHAPTER FOUR

STRESSED OUT!

"MY SPIRIT IS OVERWHELMED WITHIN ME. MY HEART WITHIN ME IS DISTRESSED."

Psalm 143:4, NKJV

"Your eyes were bigger than your stomach," my mother would gently scold, as I brought my half-filled plate to her at the kitchen sink. This was a frequent occurrence at the big family get-togethers in our home. Every few years, it would be "our turn" to host a get-together, and my father's brothers would bring their families out to our place. The meal was always potluck, for my aunts were all good cooks and my uncles were all good eaters.

The buffet in our dining room would be lined with huge serving dishes of steaming food. The kids would get to go through the line first, and I would take liberally from all my favorite dishes. One of my cousins always took one dinner roll and several scoops of black olives—he was a fussy eater. As I took my seat at the card table in the kitchen, he'd wave his olive-capped fingers at the others. The children's table was always noisy, and with all the excitement and chatter, most of my food would go untouched. The dishes were gathered up and washed before Aunt Mary Jean's

CLEARING THE COBWEBS

How did your mom fix your hair when you were little? Was there a comfortable everyday style? Was there something more extravagant she did for special occasions?

bars were uncovered for dessert, so my lack of appetite was always discovered. Since wasting food was looked down upon, the scolding always came. "Your eyes were bigger than your stomach."

Many of us scoop more onto our plates than we can handle in a day. It all looks good. A little more couldn't hurt. But pretty soon we realize our ambitions were bigger than our time. That's when stress begins to weigh us down. Do you have too much on your plate?

1. Stress is defined as a mentally or emotionally disruptive condition occurring in response to adverse external influences. It is capable of affecting physical health, usually characterized by increased heart rate, a rise in blood pressure, muscular tension, irritability, and depression. What words would you use to describe your emotions when you are under stress?

> The last minute is how I live most of my life. I tend to downshift when I should be accelerating and vice versa. This on-the-edge habit leaves me breathless, frustrated, and a little ditzy. For some reason, in those last minutes, reality thumps me upside the head, and life finally comes into focus, which leaves me scurrying to catch up.
>
> Patsy Clairmont

2. You won't find "stress" in your Bible concordances, but some verses of Scripture give apt descriptions of the emotions that are rolling within a stressed-out woman's heart. Look at Psalm 143:4. What kinds of situations bring on these feelings in your day?

3. We get too busy, and then pay for it by our ragged emotions. Do we really need to be as busy as we are? What does Psalm 39:6 say about busyness?

4. There are times when we all feel the pressure, and stress sneaks into our lives. Maybe it was the weekend you invited the Pastor over for lunch, then realized you had signed up to bring treats to your Sunday school class, and you had to teach the two-year-olds during the Sunday morning service, too. Ach! Where does Psalm 102:1 show us to turn when we are feeling overwhelmed?

> *Don't let your life speed out of control. Live intentionally. Do something today that will last beyond your lifetime.*
>
> Barbara Johnson

5. Time is fleeting. Time is short. How are we supposed to use our time? Look in Ephesians 5:15–16.

6. I love the wording found in the New King James Version for that verse. Paul says we are to be "redeeming the time." What does that mean, "redeeming the time"?

> *I don't know about you, but I want to do more than survive life. It's not enough to just flap my wings a little before I hit the ground and get plowed under. I want to mount up like the eagle and glide over rocky crags, nest in the tallest trees, dive for nourishment in the deepest of mountain lakes, and soar on the wings of the wind.*
>
> Barbara Johnson

My daughter has long hair. Perhaps it's because I never did. My mother grew weary of the wailing and tears that accompanied a good brushing. "It hurts," I'd cry. So she set aside her comb and brought out the scissors. Actually, I was sent to the local barber, and the majority of my long tresses were lopped off. That was back in the day when the "shag" haircut was in style, and I looked like a miniature Mrs. Brady.

> For most of us, our greatest fear is running out of time. So we hurry through life trying desperately to get everything done: working overtime, eating fast food in the car, racing down the freeway. In our quest to save time, we're losing something.
>
> Luci Swindoll

So, I have let my girl's hair grow out, and it is lovely—silky blonde waves that fall to her waist. We play with different styles, barrettes, scrunchies, clips, buns, and braids. But, we are in a daily battle against tangles. "Bird's have been building nests again," or "A whole family of mice could live in here" and "My, what a rat's nest" are joking comments I have handed down from my mother. Tears well up as the comb works through a particularly tough spot, but I assure my girl that they will only get worse if we don't get rid of them.

Life is a little like that. When our schedules are tangled up, and there seems no hope of smoothing them, it's time to make some changes. For if we don't tame the tangles, they will only get worse. Then, there'll be nothing left for us but to bring out the scissors.

7. As you face a tangle of responsibilities, and you feel the tension building in your heart, where can you turn to dispel the mounting levels of stress? There's a hint in Psalm 119:143.

8. Though these suggestions may help you survive the stresses of your day, wouldn't it be nice to get rid of the stress altogether? What kind of life do you long for? Find Paul's recommendation in 1 Thessalonians 4:11.

9. A quiet life is a commendable thing, but what else does God want us to aspire to?

10. When we fight through the noise and discover the quiet life, what will be the only busyness left to us? I love the promise in Ecclesiastes 5:20.

Digging Deeper

When days become flurries of activity and stress mounts, we long for a quiet haven of peace. The following verses speak of both a longing for peace and the promise of rest.

- Psalm 55:6
- Psalm 61:2
- Psalm 107:30
- Isaiah 14:7
- Zephaniah 3:17

Ponder & Pray

As we try to keep up with all that needs doing, stress can mount until we feel frantic. Instead of getting caught in a whirlpool of busyness that sucks you down into despair, ask God for the grace to face one task at a time. Pray for peace; plead for a calm heart. Ask the Lord to lead you through your days, changing your spirit until you are marked by quietness and gentleness.

Trinkets to Treasure

Your trinket for this week is a comb, to help you untangle your strained emotions! When stresses plague you, gently smooth down your mixed emotions. Calm your fears, ease through your anger, unkink your pride. Don't be tempted to let these feelings go, because left in their tangled state, they'll only get worse. Call upon the Lord to come and work through the rat's nest in your soul. Once His work is done, you will have the quiet and gentle spirit that is so very precious in God's sight.

NOTES & PRAYER REQUESTS

CHAPTER FIVE

BLESSINGS IN DISGUISE

"KEEP ME FROM PAYING ATTENTION TO WHAT IS
WORTHLESS; BE GOOD TO ME AS YOU HAVE PROMISED."

Psalm 119:37, TEV

When someone is wrapped up in their work, it can be very difficult to get their attention. To compensate, our society has provided several means of polite interruption. Consider the gentle clearing of the throat. A quiet "ahem" is one way of letting someone know you have entered their domain and would like to speak. A short little cough often works just as well. We are taught very young to raise our hands for permission to speak in the classroom. In restaurants, we put on a hopeful look and try to catch the eye of our waitress. If that fails, we snap our fingers or wave our hands to draw her attention. A sharp whistle is useful for hailing cabs and calling dogs.

Then, there are bells. Doorbells, countertop bells you tap, handbells you swing, dinnerbells you clang with a rod. One of our local restaurants has a whole string of sleigh bells on their front door, which jingle-jangle every time the door is opened, and don't forget horns. Car horns can be

CLEARING ⊁ THE ⊁ COBWEBS

Name a few ways
God caught people's
attention in order
to speak to them
in Bible days.

blown to alert the folks ahead of you the light has turned, or blared to let someone know they've just behaved foolishly. At our Wal-Mart™, there is a bulb-horn to honk if you need assistance at the fabric-cutting counter.

So how does God get our attention? We are busy people, and bells and whistles aren't usually a part of His repertoire. Getting our attention is a tricky business!

1. Would you say you are really living, or just surviving life? What's the difference between the two?

2. Are you satisfied with your life, or do you find yourself longing for something quieter, less frenzied?

> The disturbing reality is, at times, we all appear to be running. . . running literally for our lives. We're running from responsibilities, we're running from hurtful memories, we're running from relationships that require time and discipline to repair, we're running from various fears we think may overtake us, and we're even running from knowledge of ourselves. I don't have to run to survive. As a matter of fact, I am invited to rest to survive.
>
> Marilyn Meberg

3. God resorts to outrageous means to get our attention sometimes. Moses needed his burning bush, and Jonah needed his whale. Is there a chance God is using stress to get your attention?

y children love to build things with those wooden blocks with the alphabet on them. Early on, when stacking them neatly was a challenge, they would create long low fences, or lines they called trains. But as their coordination improved, their towers soared. The oldest of them would create castles with impressive towers. They learned that in order to build a really tall building, they needed to set the blocks on a heavy book or tabletop. The carpeting had too much give, and buildings began to lean early in construction. Have you considered your foundations lately? Is your life teetering because it doesn't have a firm footing?

> *What Christ cares about is our hearts, our complete love and devotion. And He will create crisis in our lives to show us what holds us. As I looked closely at myself, I began to see I had been given a most awesome gift, the gift of crisis, to see what was in my soul.*
>
> Sheila Walsh

4. We are building our lives, too, and we must choose our foundation carefully. What does the parable in Matthew 7:24–27 teach us?

5. More advice about having a good foundation is found in 1 Timothy 6:19. Why does Paul say we need that foundation?

6. Let's back up a few verses. What does 1 Timothy 6:3 say is the foundation for a godly life?

7. In 1 Corinthians 3:10, Paul urges Christians to build on the foundation God has laid. What is his next caution?

> *I'm not kidding. Even stress can be a blessing if you know how to deal with it. Instead of asking God to get rid of it, I had to learn to neutralize its effect. I discovered that winners turn stress into something good, while losers let stress turn life into something bad. Winners see an answer for every problem, while losers see a problem for every answer. Knowing these differences and incorporating them into the way you face stress is key to keeping your dignity and peace in adversity.*
>
> Barbara Johnson

8. What has God used to catch your attention lately?

DIGGING DEEPER

Is God trying to capture your attention? It's far too easy to take God for granted in the midst of busy days. When life becomes a whirlwind of activity, we must scrutinize our foundations. That overwhelming stress in our life forces us to make a careful inspection of our plans. Let's explore some verses of Scripture that speak of our foundation.

- Proverbs 10:25 • Isaiah 28:16 • 1 Corinthians 3:11
- 2 Timothy 2:19 • 1 Peter 5:10

PONDER & PRAY

Has God been using a dissatisfaction with your hectic life to grab your attention? Pray for a clearness of understanding as you test your foundations. Have you built wisely? Do you need to renovate? Ask the Lord to guide you through the process of change that must come. Pray for assurance and peace that your choices are wise ones. He will give you joy as you build.

TRINKETS TO TREASURE

Your little treasure this week is a building block. It will serve to remind you of the life you are building and the foundation on which it is laid. When your tower begins to teeter and topples to the ground, do not dismay! The tumbledown condition of your life might just be God's invitation to rebuild! Whenever your little block catches your attention during the busyness of your day, remember that God might be trying to capture your attention, too!

NOTES & PRAYER REQUESTS

_____

_____

_____

_____

_____

_____

_____

_____

_____

_____

_____

_____

_____

_____

_____

_____

_____

_____

_____

_____

_____

CHAPTER SIX

GOOD VENTILATION

"I AM PRAYING TO YOU BECAUSE I KNOW YOU WILL ANSWER, O GOD. BEND DOWN AND LISTEN AS I PRAY."

Psalm 17:6, NLT

Emotions are interesting things. We all have them, we all are affected by them, and we all try to hide them sometimes. Those of us who cannot hide them well are subject to comments like "she wears her heart on her sleeve" or "it was written all over her face." Twitching eyebrows, clenched jaw, blushing cheeks, and pursed lips are telltale signs of our inner fluttering hearts, churning stomachs, indignant sensibilities, or raging hormones.

But emotions don't like to stay hidden for long. In subtle, or not-so-subtle, ways, we broadcast our feelings to the world. Our emotional vocabulary includes some pretty interesting phraseology. We talk about our stomach dropping out, our heart stopping, or blowing our stack. We feel down in the dumps, hopping mad, in a tizzy, all choked up, in a funk, sick at heart, swamped, and at odds with ourselves.

And when it's time for these emotions to come gushing out, they take many forms: temper tantrums, endless ranting, sleepless nights, mood

CLEARING ⚐ THE ⚐ COBWEBS

Some gals holler, others get very, very quiet. How do you let people know you are mad? Personally, I'm a cupboard door slammer!

swings, critical attitudes, blind rages, constant complaining, pity parties, and hissy fits. Unfortunately, all of these very popular options are not appropriate for Christian women. Proverbs 29:11 says, "Only a fool vents all his feelings, but a wise man holds them back" (NKJV). But that doesn't mean we should bottle it all up. No, God knows we just need to release some of that inner turbulence—carefully!

1. Who is someone you trust, someone who will never tell what comes up during an angry spat, someone who can listen with understanding—someone you can vent to? How has this person helped you?

> We can sigh about things, or we can laugh. Both these responses release pressure, but which is the most fun? We laugh so we won't scream. Whatever it is probably won't go away, so we might as well live and laugh through it.
>
> Barbara Johnson

2. Though it comes most naturally to let off steam in the form of angry words or bitter complaints, laughter is a wonderful alternative! Have you ever turned a frustrating event into a funny story? Try that here!

3. What does Solomon say about a sense of humor? Look at Proverbs 17:22.

4. When we choose to release some of our frustrations with laughter, we allow others around us to relax and join in the chuckle. A woman who is willing to find the funny in her days is unmistakable. What does she look like according to Proverbs 15:13?

*I*t's not hard to spot complainers, with their furrowed brows and down-turned lips. Their ways of venting can be downright depressing to those who are forced to endure them. Whenever my husband is faced with one of our children in such a state of facial disarray, he interrupts the coming tirade and commands, "put your eyebrows up." It might sound silly, but it works. It's *very* hard to maintain a frown while arching your eyebrows. Immediately, our child's expressions would dissolve into a smile and a giggle. Then, their concerns can be related without the stormy face. Try it!

5. Our Lord is even better than any earthly friend. He's available to us whenever we feel the need to unburden our hearts. David said, "Each morning I bring my requests to You and wait expectantly" (Ps. 5:3, NLT). What else does David say in Psalm 55:2?

6. Why does God make an ideal listener in our times of turmoil? Look at 1 Peter 5:7.

> *Perhaps it seems to you that you are at the breaking point. I urge you in the name of the Lord to throw yourself on Him, to hide yourself under His wings. Don't give up. You have come too far. The road ahead may look bleak, but trust in God. It is the way home.*
>
> Sheila Walsh

> *As you walk through your days,*
> *you encounter various situations*
> *in life that may trouble you. If*
> *you're like me there are decisions*
> *that must be made that seem*
> *bigger than I have the capacity*
> *to handle. At times like these we*
> *can either quiver in our boots*
> *and become paralyzed by that*
> *"deer caught in the headlights"*
> *phenomenon, or we can talk to*
> *the One who is able to calm our*
> *apprehensions and fears and give*
> *us courage to move ahead with a*
> *heart of confidence and assurance.*
> *In other words, we can pray.*
>
> Luci Swindoll

7. When you are facing a tough day, how do you feel after you pray about it?

8. Read Jeremiah 29:11–14. What does God promise concerning our prayers?

> *The truth is that every day has*
> *its share of stress. When you*
> *feel like an aerosol can because*
> *you are under too much pressure,*
> *find a listening ear to act as a*
> *safety valve. Throw a pity party*
> *for your friends so you can all*
> *get it out of your system at once.*
> *Drown your fears in compassion*
> *for each other and then rise up*
> *and give yourselves a great big*
> *hug. Encourage each other to*
> *hang on and hang in there!*
>
> Barbara Johnson

DIGGING DEEPER

In the midst of our fears, our worries, and our stresses, God encourages us to call for Him. He has made Himself available to us 24/7 at no charge. We won't get a busy signal or a voice mailbox. He's right there, waiting for us. Here are some verses to encourage you. All of them invite us to call on God.

- Psalm 50:15
- Psalm 55:16
- Psalm 91:15
- Psalm 116:2
- Jeremiah 33:3

PONDER & PRAY

When your heart is troubled this week, or your fears and frustrations threaten to overwhelm you, turn to God. Pour it all out, and feel the relief of a good venting. He will lift those burdens right off your mind. This week, too, pray for God's strength to pray, smile, and even laugh in the midst of your emotional turmoil. Ask God to give you some perspective, to inspire you with good storytelling, and to help you release your tensions with a hearty chuckle.

TRINKETS TO TREASURE

Your trinket to treasure for this week is a smiley face. Let that cheerful little icon serve to remind you that even the most frustrating event in your day can become a source of merriment to the gal with a good sense of humor. Don't let anger and resentment find a foothold in your heart. Learn to laugh at the little troubles that face you.

NOTES & PRAYER REQUESTS

CHAPTER SEVEN

I Know Whom I Have Believed

"As for me, I trust in You, O Lord; I say, 'You are my God.'"

Psalm 31:14, NKJV

o dating and marriage have anything to do with each other? Even though the one sometimes leads to the other, they are two very different worlds. The whole thing makes me laugh. Think about it. When we meet the man of our dreams, we want so badly for him to like us. So, we work hard to look like the girl of *his* dreams. Whenever he sees us, we are lookin' good—hairspray, mascara, nail polish, perfume, the works! We smile a lot, laugh at all his little jokes, and are fascinated by his conversation.

Some may call this false advertising, but it goes both ways. Mr. Wonderful is also careful to always be clean. He showers and shaves, wears clothes that coordinate, matches his socks, and keeps his fingernails clean. The more serious man has also been known to plan an entire evening's entertainment, bring flowers, tip well, write poetry, and make sweet little compliments.

Clearing ⊀ the ⊱ Cobwebs

Did you ever play "hide the button" when you were a child? What did your favorite hiding-button look like? Mine was pink with a white stripe around the edge! What were your cleverest hiding places?

Both believe they have discovered the most perfect person in the world, and so they take the plunge. They get married. They feel secure. They relax. He sees her without makeup, in a bad mood, during *that* time of the month. She finds out he makes indiscrete noises, picks his nose, and wants a truck. Newlyweds are always shocked, but adjusting to reality is just a part of getting to know one another—of becoming *one*.

It's tricky to really get to know people. We hold back our true feelings so as not to offend. We guard our opinions to stay out of tiresome arguments. And we suspect everybody else is doing it, too. With so much subterfuge going on, real friendships are slow to form. After all, how can you trust someone you do not know?

1. Do you trust God? In what ways do you trust Him with *everything* in your life?

2. Have you ever been disappointed by somebody? Have you ever had your trust betrayed? All of us have, at some time or another. What does Psalm 118:8 caution?

> God speaks to us clearly. He means what He says. What He says He'll provide, we can count on that. When He promises peace, wisdom, strength, or comfort, they are ours. God imparts His word and keeps it. His words matter! I find tremendous comfort in that.
>
> Luci Swindoll

3. Why is it better to trust God? Psalm 9:10 gives a very good reason.

4. Look at Proverbs 3:5. When is it the hardest to trust God? What circumstances have made it difficult for you to maintain your confidence in Him?

> *Our God is the all-knowing One who sees our scars, our secrets, and our strength. Our wounds and shame are His affair, and He knows just how much trouble we can stand.*
>
> Barbara Johnson

5. Do you believe God? In what ways do you trust Him to follow through on all His promises to you?

6. How should that belief affect your everyday life? What about your fears? What about worry? Stress?

7. Trusting God has its benefits. Secure in the knowledge of His love and care, we are not easily shaken by our circumstances. But there is another wonderful result of our confidence in God. What does David say about this in Psalm 73:28?

*D*id you like to play hide-and-seek when you were little? My sister and I loved the game, and our house was full of hiding places. Old houses always have many great nooks and crannies, and we could spend a whole morning at the game. The hider would squirm into some distant corner, and the seeker would turn the house upside down trying to find her. It never really took long to discover a hiding place, though. For some reason, the hider couldn't keep quiet. We would wiggle and giggle and peek out of our spot to see if the seeker was getting close. Hiding was great, but the real fun was in being found!

Have you ever felt like you were in a game of hide-and-seek with God? There are those times in our lives when we feel like God has hidden Himself from us. We feel so very alone, and we long to find Him again. In the Bible, God often welcomes us to seek after Him. And He wants to be found, too! God has promised that if we seek Him, we will find Him!

I turn to the Word of God to remind myself who God is and who He longs to be in our lives. He longs to give us what we cannot drum up for ourselves: courage beyond our capacity, to give us peace, to give us a quietness of heart, to give us wisdom, to give us the proper types of responses in the appropriate situations. There is nothing wrong with being a little knee-knocking uneasy. Many times life brings us things that will cause that type of reaction. It's when fear begins to paralyze us that it becomes inappropriate and unhelpful and truly unnecessary. And so I go into the Word of God to remind myself who God is and who He longs to be in my life.

Patsy Clairmont

8. We have already stated it is hard to trust someone you do not know. So how do you get to know God? What does Jeremiah 29:13 promise?

9. What else can the seeker depend on? Look up Psalm 9:10.

10. Read 2 Samuel 22:31. How has God proven Himself to you? Are you sure of His love? Do you trust Him completely?

> God's provision is seldom on the plate at another table. When you find yourself looking at a bank balance that couldn't keep a goldfish afloat, remember who you are. Your Father knows every need before you even voice it. He knows every unexpected turn of events. We are told by Paul to be anxious about nothing. "Nothing" is a pretty conclusive word. No thing, no part, no portion.
>
> Sheila Walsh

Digging Deeper

God promises much to those who trust in Him. If you believe what He says is true, then take the leap of faith to live that way. Here are several verses that deal with trusting God. Allow them to strengthen your confidence in your Savior.

- Psalm 18:2
- Psalm 31:14
- Psalm 34:22
- Psalm 37:5
- Nahum 1:7

PONDER & PRAY

If God seems to be hiding from you lately, take this next week to earnestly seek Him. What joy you will have when you find Him! As you get to know the Lord even better this week, pray that He will help you to trust Him. Release into His hands all the little cares and worries that plague your day. He will prove Himself to be faithful in every detail.

TRINKETS TO TREASURE

Honesty, trustworthiness, dependability, loyalty, faithfulness—have you ever heard the old expression describing a person who displays all these qualities? They are said to be "true blue." Maybe that's why brides are supposed to carry "something old, something new, something borrowed, and something *blue*" on their wedding day. God is true blue. So this week's trinket is something blue, to remind you God is as good as His Word. It is a bright blue button! Use it to play "hide the button" with your kids, or put it next to your calendar at work. It will remind you that God will be found by those who seek Him!

NOTES & PRAYER REQUESTS

CHAPTER EIGHT

A Promise Is a Promise

"Without wavering, let us hold tightly to the hope we say we have, for God can be trusted to keep His promise."

Hebrews 10:23

ne of the best ways to get to know God is to seek Him out through His Word. He has made many promises to you, and everything He has promised will come to be. This chapter is dedicated to exploring just a few of God's precious promises to you. Look up each of these scriptures, and then put the promise you find in those verses into your own words below it.

CLEARING ⟋ THE ⟍ COBWEBS

As a child, did you have a little ritual to seal a promise or make a pact—secret handshakes, crossing your heart, a little pledge you repeated?

1. Psalm 31:19–20

2. Isaiah 43:2

> Just as my blind great-grandfather, Daddy Harrell, trusted me to lead him from place to place without fear of falling or being run over by a car, he taught me to trust God by turning over to Him my fears and anxieties. His remedy for my fear was Psalm 23:4: "Even though I walk through the valley of the shadow of death, I will fear no evil, for You are with me; Your rod and Your staff, they comfort me." He recited that verse to me often.
>
> Thelma Wells

3. James 4:8

4. Jeremiah 24:7

5. Psalm 10:17

6. 2 Corinthians 12:9–10

7. Isaiah 41:13

8. Deuteronomy 7:9

9. 1 Corinthians 1:8–9

10. Isaiah 26:3–4

11. Psalm 66:19

12. 2 Thessalonians 1:6–7

13. Hebrews 4:3

> *When God believes in you,*
> *your situation is never hopeless.*
> *When He walks with you, you*
> *are never alone. When God*
> *in on your side, you can never,*
> *ever lose. So don't be afraid of*
> *tomorrow—God is already there.*
>
> Barbara Johnson

14. 2 Chronicles 16:9

15. Psalm 116:1

16. John 14:1

17. Hebrews 6:10–11

18. Psalm 55:22

> *Courage and fear—those two attributes are strange bedmates. It would seem impossible to experience both of them at the same time, yet I believe that's the challenge of the Christian life. Fear tells us that life is unpredictable, anything can happen, but faith replies quietly, "Yes, but God is in control."*
>
> Sheila Walsh

19. Isaiah 46:4

20. Hebrews 6:18–19

21. Jude 24

22. 2 Thessalonians 2:16–17

23. Matthew 7:7–8

24. Isaiah 54:10

25. 1 Peter 1:4–5

26. Zephaniah 3:17

27. Joshua 1:9

28. Isaiah 54:5

29. Psalm 91:11

> *There are times you might be so fearful that all you can say is, "Lord, I'm scared. Please give me peace because I'm placing my trust in you. I know you can meet me right here. Please do!" And He will. He will enter into your mind and calm you with His presence.*
>
> Luci Swindoll

30. 1 John 2:25

Ponder & Pray

This week, as you pore over God's Word and seek Him in prayer, may God's promises leap off the page for you! Ask the Lord to show you His promises, and ask Him to strengthen your faith to believe Him. Choose a few promises that speak to your deepest needs and repeat them to yourself often. Commit them to memory and speak them aloud with confidence. God cannot lie. God will keep His word. A promise is a promise.

Trinkets to Treasure

Every promise in God's Word will come to pass. In fact, Jesus said that the stars, moon, and earth itself would come to an end before even the smallest letter of the Scriptures is left unfulfilled (Matt. 5:18). So let us take the stars for our trinket this week. The stars should always encourage us, for as long as they sparkle in the sky, God's still keeping His promises to us. Did you know He even has names for all the stars (Ps. 147:4)? He'll have a new name for you someday, too (Rev. 2:17)!

NOTES & PRAYER REQUESTS

Two Little Letters

"Let your 'yes' be 'yes,' and your 'no,' 'no.'"

Matthew 5:37, NKJV

When I was a newlywed, my husband and I rented a small apartment just up the hill from the seminary he was attending. While he tackled ancient languages, systematic theology, and principles of church growth, I tackled piles of laundry, dirty dishes, and soiled diapers. He was weighed down with a full course load and working as many hours as he could to make ends meet. Then came the perfect opportunity to earn just a little extra money. One of the young men at the school was also a new daddy, but his wife was back to working full-time. Could I watch his little boy for the hour or so he was in class?

What could be better? The child was brought to my door every morning, and picked back up in under two hours. I could earn a little extra money, and I was doing the father a great favor. I agreed. Promptly on Monday morning, eight-month old Caleb was deposited in our living room. He came equipped with a car seat, a playpen, a pacifier, and a diaper bag the size of a steamer trunk. Unfortunately, Caleb was a screamer.

Clearing the Cobwebs

Remember the old saying "act in haste, repent at leisure"? Have there been times when you've agreed to take something on, only to regret doing it later?

> Life often overtakes me. I remember boohooing on my friend Ruthann's shoulder about my complicated lifestyle. It seemed my calendar was careening out of control, turning my joyful journey into a jarring one. Ruthann, a wordsmith with a masterful vocabulary and exacting enunciation, decided I needed to expand my vocabulary. She taught me the word no—a one-syllable, two-letter powerhouse that prevents us from being victimized by life's pressures and turmoil. I'd heard the word previously, but I just wasn't proficient in its use.
>
> Patsy Clairmont

The moment his harried father left the apartment, his son sent up a piercing wail that made me shudder. I rocked him, I walked him, I sang to him, I checked his diaper, I coaxed him to take a bottle, I offered him his pacifier, and nothing worked. Poor Caleb was inconsolable. I was a brand-new mom, lacking experience and confidence. I had no idea how else to help him. In the end, I set the shrieking child in his playpen and took my own baby into our bedroom. I let him cry.

As the weeks went by, Caleb never warmed to his early morning visits to our apartment. For the rest of the semester, he would scream for a solid hour. And all the while I lay on my bed in the other room, wishing I had never agreed to babysit. I've never forgotten that awful experience, and I have learned since then to consider much more carefully before I say "yes." Even a small commitment can become a source of emotional strain that seems to dampen the rest of your day and make you dread tomorrow!

1. Do you have trouble saying no? What makes it so hard to turn people down?

2. Is it wise to say yes to everything that comes your way? Of course not! Paul gives Christians some good advice in Ephesians 5:15. What is it?

3. Many of the things women are asked to take on are good things. Special projects at work, PTA, neighborhood get-togethers, fundraisers, babysitting, special events, little league, garden clubs, aerobics class, bake sales—nobody could say these things are bad in and of themselves. But we cannot do it all; so how do we decide what is best? Wouldn't it be nice to know something was not only good, but also *perfect* for us? What does Paul say is perfect in Romans 12:2?

4. From the Bible, we know God has a plan for us and a purpose in everything that happens to us. We know God is at work in our lives, but *why*? Check out Philippians 2:13.

5. You have been seeking God and establishing your trust in Him. Have you also consulted with God about His will and your plans? Look at Deuteronomy 10:12. What does God want you to do?

> I've heard people say, "If you want anything done right, you have to do it yourself." I used to say that, too, until I realized I didn't have a life because I had so many fires to put out. The stress was overwhelming. My rationalizations for why I needed to be the one to do all those tasks was fast disappearing. I needed help.
>
> Thelma Wells

s a child, I was always a fussy eater, picking and choosing my way through a meal. Some folks are described as using their forks like a shovel, but mine was a finely tuned instrument for dissecting casseroles. From the depths of a dish concocted of hamburger, cheese, and noodles, I could find the tiny squares of mushrooms that had entered via a can of cream of mushroom soup. I lined them up on the edge of my plate!

Christians need to be picky, too. We can't just shovel in everything the world dishes up. Sure, a lot of it is good stuff, but let's not be hasty! God warns us to be circumspect. He wants us to access our opportunities carefully, be choosey, be selective, and be cautious. If God is leading you into something new, He will give us both the peace to accept it and the strength to accomplish it!

> *To do too much is as dangerous as to do nothing at all. Both modes prevent us from savoring our moments. One causes me to rush right past the best of life without recognizing or basking in it, and the other finds me sitting quietly as life rushes past me.*
>
> Patsy Clairmont

6. Our wisest course in this busy world is to keep our focus and say no to anything that does not keep us heading towards our ultimate goal. Have a plan and stick to it. Do you have goals? What are they?

> *Perhaps some of you, like me, are missing out on recreational activity that has no purpose other than to give a needed respite from our task-oriented lives. Wouldn't it be fun occasionally to produce nothing, accomplish nothing, and contribute to nothing? The possibilities for nothing are endless.*
>
> Marilyn Meberg

7. When we learn to say no to all the choices that surround us, we suddenly have time to catch our breath, to think, to rest in the Lord, and to pray. It actually feels like a *quiet* life. What one thing would you choose to do if you knew you had a week full of quiet evenings ahead of you?

8. The tricky thing about saying no is that once you have your life in hand, you start to feel like you could take on more. After all, you are rested and ready for a challenge. In your self-confidence, it's easy to start saying yes again before seeking God's will in some new venture. What does James 4:15 say about this?

9. When it comes to saying no, you need to hang in there! God will bless your efforts to pursue His perfect path. What promise are we given in Hebrews 10:36?

> *We all know what it feels like to be at rest. And we all long for that more sane lifestyle rather than being overwhelmed. But are we willing to leave the press long enough to lie down in the soothing green pastures and to be led by the still waters of His provision? That, my friend, is not resort living but restored living. And each of us needs it.*
>
> Patsy Clairmont

DIGGING DEEPER

In our hearts, we long for those words, "Well done, good and faithful servant," to be spoken to us. We want to please and glorify God. We want to do His will. So what is God's will? Several Scriptures give us a glimpse of His will. Let's explore them.

- 1 Peter 4:2
- 1 Thessalonians 5:18
- Mark 3:35
- 1 Peter 2:15
- 1 John 5:14

PONDER & PRAY

This week, ask the Lord to help you see your life with new clarity. Are there opportunities to which you should begin saying no? Pray for discernment, to tell the difference between things that are merely *good* and those things that are *best*. Pray for a new focus and the ability to decide if the things that come your way will work towards your goals or against them. Guard your time this week, and treat it as precious. Then, when God gives you an avenue of service, do that thing with all your heart!

TRINKETS TO TREASURE

In an effort to guard our time, it is often necessary to "just say no!" This week's trinket to treasure is an eye-catching reminder of those two very necessary little letters—N-O! It's the universal symbol for no. A red circle with a slash through it. Hang it on your refrigerator, by your telephone, or on your calendar. When all those wonderful opportunities come your way, your little "no" symbol will remind you to consider your goals, weigh your responsibilities, and contemplate the consequences *before* making a reply.

Notes & Prayer Requests

CHAPTER TEN

SETTING THE PACE

"YOU ALSO ASPIRE TO LEAD A QUIET LIFE, TO MIND YOUR OWN BUSINESS, AND TO WORK WITH YOUR OWN HANDS, AS WE COMMANDED YOU."

1 Thessalonians 4:11, NKJV

Nothing's like the good old days, or so I've been told. Communication has gone beyond the old-fashioned wall-mounted telephone to smartphones with wifi–and the technology keeps increasing. Things are noisier now. The background of our life is filled with the chugging of a washing machine, the whooshing of a dishwasher, the ding-dong of doorbells, the bleeps and booms of electronic games, the wail of passing sirens, the chatter of talk radio, beeping scanners at the grocery store, the rumble of road construction crews, the canned laughter of television sitcoms, elevator music, and even smartphones that play "Ode to Joy." And in the midst of this hubbub, we come across an ancient verse of Scripture that says, "Aspire to lead a quiet life."

So we are to live a quiet life, are we? Does that mean we need to pack up our families and move out into the distant hills and live on homegrown vegetables and goat's milk for the rest of our lives? Of course not. Quiet lives are not defined by quiet

CLEARING 🔏 THE 🔖 COBWEBS

How many people are in your circle of influence? How many people do you come into regular contact with, giving you an opportunity to say a kind word or offer encouragement? Who are they?

surroundings. We *are* to be women with a quiet and gentle spirit, aspiring to lead quiet lives, but just what does quiet *mean*?

1. The dictionary defines "quiet" as being calm, untroubled, and free of turmoil and agitation. How would you compare this sort of attitude to a life bothered by fear, worry, or stress?

> I know I want to be more wise than I am today. That means I'll have to use my time wisely, invest myself discerningly, and savor the flavor of every delicious moment assigned to me.
>
> Patsy Clairmont

2. What is going on right now that robs the quiet from your life?

3. When we go on a diet, we want to lose weight badly enough to give up eating sweets. We understand hot fudge sundaes prevent us from reaching our goal, so we avoid them. How badly do you want a quiet life? What would you have to give up?

ometimes, the Christian life involves a lot of hard work, but there are always times of quiet rest for each of us. Have you ever been to the performance of a large symphony orchestra? In the beginning, as you find your seats and browse through your program, the members of the orchestra begin to slip into their seats. One by one, the black-clad musicians warm up, tuning their instruments in preparation to play. The sound is a jumbled nonsense. Then, the conductor arrives. All eyes turn to him as he raises his baton. The music begins, softly. You lean forward to catch the melody. The measures flow past; the sound builds to a crescendo, every instrument doing its part. It is beautiful.

If you watch the orchestra pit carefully, you notice a couple of things. Though every seat is filled, not all the musicians are playing at every moment. As the conductor leads them through the music, some sections play, but others are at rest. When greater sound is called for, many are busy. When the softest movements are underway, a single instrument may have the spotlight. Yet all the orchestra members keep their eye on the conductor's baton.

The church is like that orchestra. We all keep our eyes on the Conductor, awaiting His direction. At times, we work hard, and the music of our lives is glorious. At other times, we are allowed to rest. Others take up the song. Life has that sort of ebb and flow. Whether you are giving your all right now, or are in a season of attentive rest, quietly waiting your turn, you are an important part of a larger group. And the result of our woven lives is beautiful, and it all glorifies God.

4. Let's look at the rest of that verse from 1 Thessalonians 4:11. Paul also encourages those Christians to mind their own business. Why do you think that is important within the church? Aren't we supposed to be caring for one another?

> When I hear people complaining, I often think, "They can't distinguish between a mere inconvenience and a major catastrophe." Think of the pain and conflict we would spare ourselves, the stress we would forego, if we just realized mere inconveniences could be survived.
>
> Luci Swindoll

5. Gossip, rumors, and false assumptions do more damage within the church than anything else. Even Jesus warns about meddling in others' lives when we should be tending to our own (Matt. 7:3–4). What does Paul say about such busybodies in 2 Thessalonians 3:11 and 1 Timothy 5:13?

6. Setting the pace of our life has a lot to do with adjusting our attitudes, so while we're on the subject of watching our tongues, let's mention complaining. James 5:9 says, "Do not grumble against one another, brethren, lest you be condemned" (NKJV). One grumbler can influence an entire group for the worst. Paul gives us a better pattern. What do Ephesians 4:2–3 and Colossians 3:13 tell us to do instead?

7. Have you ever heard the adage, "Idle hands are the devil's playground"? Why do you suppose Paul encourages Christians to work with their own hands in 1 Thessalonians 4:11?

8. Does Paul's advice mean we should avoid contact with one another? Of course not! Have you ever noticed that many of the commands we are given in the Bible and many of the gifts and talents we receive from the Holy Spirit are only useful in group settings? What does 1 Peter 4:10 say?

9. We Christians are to be working together in harmony, creating a beautiful example of love and unity. Ephesians 4:32 says, "Be kind to one another, tenderhearted, forgiving one another, just as God in Christ forgave you" (NKJV). We are a part of a caring community. What does Hebrews 10:24 encourage us to do?

10. We are supposed to live a quiet life, but we are not to become hermits—religious recluses. At the same time, we are to show caring concern for our Christian brothers and sisters, but we are not to become busybodies and meddlers. In setting the pace for your life, which of those two paths would you be more likely to take? What can you do to keep a balance between the two?

> *We don't always have time for grand departures to wonderful retreats or resorts where we can be refreshed and renewed. That is why I treasure small harbors. They are all around us waiting to let us catch our breath before the next wind carries us away.*
>
> Sheila Walsh

DIGGING DEEPER

It's easy to get so caught up in organizing our own lives that we neglect our place in the community of Christ. When our lives are too busy, that doesn't necessarily mean we should pull out of our involvement in our church. Though we need to pull our lives together so that worry and stress can be placed into God's capable hand, we cannot forget one another. The Bible is filled with passages that tell of Christians' love and care for one another. Here are just a few of the passages.

- John 13:34–35
- Romans 12:10
- Galatians 6:2
- 1 Thessalonians 5:11
- 1 Peter 4:8–10

PONDER & PRAY

Pray this week for a quiet life—one unbothered by worries or caught up in busyness. Stifle gossip and bite your tongue if you feel a grumble rising up. Ask the Lord to help you pursue His will each day with a quiet and gentle spirit. Then ask for Him to show you ways to touch others who are looking harried and haggard. It doesn't take much to give a friend a little lift! Encourage one another this week.

TRINKETS TO TREASURE

This week's little treasure is a tongue-in-cheek reminder that we need to be living a quiet life. It's a chance to stay home, mind your own business, and work with your hands. You'll need to clear a little space on the kitchen counter, and find a big mixing bowl. You'll get to tie on an apron and fill your living space with tantalizing aromas. It's the recipe for "hermits"—an old-fashioned drop cookie. While the whole cookie-making process might bless you, it's not a gift to hoard to yourself. No religious recluses allowed! Take your fresh cookies around to all your friends and neighbors, and enjoy those hermits *together*!

NOTES & PRAYER REQUESTS

CHAPTER ELEVEN

STEADY AS SHE GOES!

"NOT THAT I HAVE ALREADY ATTAINED, OR AM ALREADY PERFECTED; BUT I PRESS ON, THAT I MAY LAY HOLD OF THAT FOR WHICH CHRIST JESUS HAS ALSO LAID HOLD OF ME."

Philippians 3:12, NKJV

We lived in a farming community, and farm cats were plentiful. So, when we were quite small, my Dad found us a couple of kittens for pets. They increased and multiplied greatly, and a new litter arrived every spring. My mother was not exactly fond of these critters. She called them vultures and would shoo them off the porch with her broom. At one point, we had more than twenty cats. They would all drape themselves across our front step, sunning themselves, and waiting for table scraps. Mom declared that enough was enough. We could keep a few tomcats for mousing, but the rest would have to go.

We gave away free kittens. We donated several adult cats to the surrounding farms. The front step was cleared. Mother was pleased. Then, Peaches came back. Peaches was a particularly fruitful mama kitty with orange fur and yellow eyes, known to give both spring and fall litters. She'd walked home from the farm where she'd

CLEARING THE COBWEBS

Have you ever taken on a long-term project—a quilt, a cross-stitch sampler, a Bible study program, a scrapbook, a weight-loss program, an educational class— that took a long time to finish? How long did it take? How did it feel when you finally completed it?

73

> Now is usually when I need my help. That's because I tend to let things—activities, demands, mail, dishes, bills, laundry, telephone messages, people's expectations—pile up until I'm howling for help and blubbering the blues.
>
> Patsy Clairmont

been dropped off—five miles away. It was amazing! Such devotion! Such determination!

But Mom was adamant. She would have to go back. This time, Dad called a farmer who lived a good ten miles away. Peaches was accepted into a new barn on a dairy farm. But two weeks later, she was back. We were astonished. We were amused. She was one very persistent cat. In the end, we had to take Peaches to a farm that was across a wide river to keep her from returning. She settled down there, and blessed that farm with many a litter of orange kittens with wide yellow eyes.

Sometimes our fears are like that. We pray. We repent. We turn those fears over. We set them at God's feet and walk away, only to find them back on our doorstep the next day. Though we give up our worries, they slowly make their way back to us, surprising us with their presence after long weeks of absence. What do we do when fears and worries start to worm their way back into our lives?

1. We all want to move forward in our Christian walk, making steady progress on a smooth path. But sometimes the hill is steep, and our footing begins to slip. Do you sometimes feel like you're taking two steps forward, and one step back? What do you do in these situations?

2. When our prayers go unanswered, or our worst fears are realized, one of our first reactions is to ask, "Doesn't God love me anymore?" "Didn't I do it right?" "Am I a bad Christian?" What does 1 Peter 1:6–9 say about these trials we face?

3. Whether you stumble over some rock in the road or trip over your own shoelaces, keep on walking. Don't give up! Have patience in the process. What does James 1:2–4 encourage us to do?

4. When a huge crisis comes into our lives, we often find the gumption to face it bravely and with grace. However, when little things go wrong in our days, we've met our match. Do you have trouble maintaining your calm in the face of daily interruptions, misunderstandings, conflicts, and messes? What do you do when this happens?

5. Paul says "everything else is worthless when compared with the priceless gain of knowing Christ Jesus my Lord" (Phil. 3:8, NLT). That's the Bible's own version of "Don't sweat the small stuff!" Never lose faith! What does 1 John 5:4–5 declare?

> *My friend, remember to take this life one day at a time. When several days attack you, don't give up. A successful woman takes the bricks the devil throws at her and uses them to lay a firm foundation. We all need enough trials to challenge us, enough challenges to strengthen us, and enough strength to do our part in making this a better place to live and love.*
>
> Barbara Johnson

*M*ost of our days are filled with tasks we have to redo again and again. We wash dishes, only to wash those same dishes again at the next meal. We launder the same clothes over and over. We re-vacuum rooms. We re-mow the lawn. We re-dust our rooms. We re-wash our hair. We re-apply lipstick. Sometimes we wish the things we did would just stay done!

These same kinds of maintenance issues come into play in our spiritual lives. We must re-read the Scriptures over and over. We must confess our sins to the Lord on a regular basis. And just when we think we have given all of our cares over to God, we find them sneaking back. That's part of being human.

Don't be surprised if you have to deal with your fears and frustrations more than once. But don't feel defeated, as if you didn't get it right the first time. Deal with your heart before your worries can take hold again.

> What gets in the way of my being able to live in the moment is trying to do too many things at once, forgetting that if I just pick up the first thing first and the second thing next, I'll get things done I have to get done. Instead I tend to start feeling cluttered or panicked that I can't possibly finish it all, and I don't get anything done right until I slow down long enough to focus on one task at a time.
>
> Thelma Wells

6. How well do you know yourself? Can you tell when you're in danger of a panic attack or an angry outburst, or do they sneak up on you? What does James 1:23–25 recommend for self-examination?

7. It's easy to fall into the trap of bad reactions. We make a disgusted "tsk," roll our eyes, sigh deeply, furrow our brows, glare menacingly, raise our voices, stomp our feet, use "gentled down" curses like "good grief" and "rats," and generally make a scene. It isn't pretty, and all the while we *know* we shouldn't be reacting this way. What does Proverbs 19:11 urge the wise to do?

8. When it comes right down to it, there is only one way to get to know God enough to trust Him. There is only one way to deepen our relationship with Him. There is only one way we can know how to please God. There is only one place we can turn to hear His voice. What does Jesus say about this is in John 8:31?

> *A calmer faith. That's the quiet place within us where we don't get whiplash every time life tosses us a curve. Where we relax (versus stew, sweat, and swear) in the midst of an answerless season. Where we are not intimidated or persuaded by other people's agendas but moved only by Him. Where we weep in repentance, sleep in peace, live in fullness, and sing of victory.*
>
> Patsy Clairmont

9. *Abide.* Now there's a word full of cozy connotations. Jesus calls us to abide in Him (John 15:4), and the closeness of that kind of a relationship has been a comfort to our lonely hearts on many a dreary day. However, John mentions another kind of abiding. What does 1 John 2:24 urge?

10. With an abiding faith, we are assured victorious lives. How would you define victory? What does Revelation 21:7 say?

> *The best advice in order to face each day is this: Hope for the best, get ready for the worst, and then take whatever God sends.*
>
> Barbara Johnson

DIGGING DEEPER

Women of faith have need of endurance in this Christian life. We have to hang in there and depend upon God. He promises great things to those who are able to overcome. The book of Revelation holds several of these precious promises. Let's look them over!

- Revelation 2:7
- Revelation 2:11
- Revelation 2:17
- Revelation 2:26
- Revelation 3:5
- Revelation 3:12
- Revelation 3:21

PONDER & PRAY

Make yourself the subject of study this week. Notice what "pushes your buttons" or leads to anxious thoughts. Ask the Lord to help you understand yourself better. Then pray for the Spirit to interrupt your disgruntled frame of mind before it reaches the reaction stage. Depend on His strength to calm your fears and cool your anger. Abide in His Word this week, and abide in Jesus. Pray for His perspective on little inconveniences, a changed attitude, and a transformed heart.

TRINKETS TO TREASURE

A famous fable is the tale of the "Tortoise and the Hare," in which an over-confident bunny is caught napping while a plodding turtle finishes the race. Your trinket this week is a turtle! No matter how daunting your day may be, keep plodding away. Though others may mock your path or your goal, pursue the race set before you with unswerving purpose. When you look at your little turtle buddy, remember that the going may seem very slow, but your Heavenly Father has equipped you to reach the finish line. Your victory will be a great surprise to those who tried to discourage you—you may even surprise yourself!

NOTES & PRAYER REQUESTS

PERFECT PEACE

"PEACE I LEAVE WITH YOU, MY PEACE I GIVE TO YOU;
NOT AS THE WORLD GIVES DO I GIVE YOU. LET NOT YOUR
HEART BE TROUBLED, NEITHER LET IT BE AFRAID."

John 14:27, NKJV

Of all God's gifts to His believers, peace has proven the most difficult for the enemy to counterfeit. Lust can masquerade as love. Pride can hide in a cloak of humility or generosity. Temporary happiness will often look more appealing than true joy. Then there's peace. You either have it or you don't!

What is peace? We all know what peace should feel like, even if it has been a while since we've had that peaceful, easy feeling. We long for that calmness, serenity, and quiet confidence that comes from a truly peaceful heart.

All of us want peace. Peace with God. World peace. Peace of mind. Peace that passes understanding. Peace is a little foretaste of heaven. We sing about peace in our worship services. "Let there be peace on earth and let it begin with me." "I've got peace like a river." "Sleep in heavenly peace." "Peace on earth, good will to men." "When peace like a river attendeth my way." How we long to be able to say, "It is well with my soul!"

CLEARING ↗ THE ↖ COBWEBS

Describe a time when you faced a difficult choice to make, but you had peace in your decision.

1. Studying the names of God gives us the thrill of getting to know Him better. He has many names throughout the Scriptures. What name is found in Romans 15:33 and again in Philippians 4:9?

2. Ephesians 2:14 declares that Jesus Christ is our peace. What is one of His well-known titles from the Scriptures, found in Isaiah 9:6?

> *None of us can avoid the gray skies and dreariness of life. At times we get absolutely drenched with troubles. But you know what? They're gonna clear up! Nothing lasts forever. The stuff we go through is only temporary. There will be lots of clearings along the way. And one day we will enjoy blue skies forever.*
>
> Barbara Johnson

3. Does peace mean freedom from conflict? No! Jesus declares that this world is full of troubles. Then why are we able to have peace, even in the midst of trials? Read John 16:33.

4. Philippians 4:7 describes God's peace as "surpassing all understanding." What does Paul mean by this?

5. What does the second half of Philippians 4:7 say peace will do?

> *If we will relinquish control of our lives and place our trust in God with absolute confidence, then the peace of God, which is beyond human understanding, will cover us, protecting our hearts and minds.*
>
> Sheila Walsh

6. What does Colossians 3:15 say about peace?

7. What should our attitude be towards peace? Do we just sit back and let the Lord pour it over us? Well, yes and no. What do Romans 14:19 and 1 Peter 3:11 urge us to do?

8. Here is our benediction—one last verse to encourage your heart. Look at Paul's words in 2 Thessalonians 3:16. How will you apply this verse to your life this week?

> *When we reach the end of our strength, wisdom, and personal resources, we enter into the beginning of His glorious provisions. And that's a wondrous place to be.*
>
> Patsy Clairmont

DIGGING DEEPER

Peace. According to Romans 5:1, we have peace with God. But that's not where it stops. Peace is one of the fruits of the Spirit, and we are to extend peace to one another. Let's explore several passages of Scripture that describe the peace that should exist among Christians.

- 1 Corinthians 14:33
- 2 Corinthians 12:11
- 1 Thessalonians 5:13
- Hebrews 12:14
- James 3:18

PONDER & PRAY

God has asked you to trust Him. He has told you not to worry. He has promised you peace. Though your life may be in a turmoil that makes the idea of peace ridiculous, remember God has promised a peace that surpasses understanding. This week, as you ponder these Scriptures, *let* God's peace rule in your heart!

TRINKETS TO TREASURE

God has given us many gifts, but only we can accept them, open them, and use them. The gift of peace is ours, and the Scriptures say we should let it rule in our hearts. This week's trinket is a crown, to serve as a reminder of just *who* and *what* is reigning in our lives. Is peace there? Is the Prince of Peace on the throne? May it always be so!

NOTES & PRAYER REQUESTS

SHALL WE REVIEW?

Every chapter has added a new trinket to your treasure trove of memories. Let's remind ourselves of the lessons they hold for us!

1. A leaf

Our days can feel as scattered as leaves. Rather than becoming a cluttered pile of dried leaves, drifting around with every breath of wind, we must become a fresh, new leaf, clinging securely to the branch. Is it time for you to "turn over a new leaf"?

2. A Night-light

A reminder that we don't have to be afraid of the dark, or anything else for that matter! We are precious to God, and He will take care of us. We can trust Him.

3. A Worry Stone

Normally, it's kept in the pocket and rubbed to release nervous tension. As Christians, we have no need of its calming effects. We can leave our smooth stone behind, knowing God can handle our worries. Rather than carrying them with us, we leave them at His feet.

4. A Comb

When stress creeps into our lives, and our emotions become a tangled mess, we can call upon the Lord to work through that rat's nest in our soul. After He's calmed our fears, eased our anger, and unkinked our pride, we'll be left with the quiet and gentle spirit that is so precious in His sight.

5. A Building Block

As we build our lives, we must consider carefully what we choose as a foundation. If the tower we've been building has begun to teeter and topple, we need to accept God's invitation to rebuild.

6. A Smiley Face

A cheerful reminder that even the most frustrating event in our day can become a source of merriment to a gal with a good sense of humor. Learn to let go of building tensions by whispering a prayer and giving a giggle.

7. A Blue Button

A true blue trinket to remind us God is as good as His Word. When we seek Him, we will surely find Him. God wants us to know Him.

8. A Star

Every promise God has made will be fulfilled, and He has said the stars will disappear from the sky before any Scripture is left undone. So every time we see our star or the twinkling sky at night, we can remember God is still keeping His promises.

9. A "No" Symbol

The familiar red circle with a slash through it is a reminder to "just say no!" Though many good opportunities may present themselves to us and our family, we must stay focused, think before we answer, and only say yes to the best.

10. A Recipe for "Hermits"

Though we aren't to become religious recluses, we are called upon to live a quiet life. This batch of cookies gives us the chance to stay at home, mind our own business, and work with our hands. Then, we can share the cookies freely in order to bless those around us!

11. A Turtle

Like the tortoise racing the hare, we must keep plodding away. Though our progress may seem slow, our Heavenly Father has equipped us to reach the finish line. Hang in there!

12. A Crown

The Bible encourages us to let peace rule in our hearts. The crown reminds us to ask ourselves just who is reigning in our lives. Is it the Prince of Peace?

LEADER'S GUIDE

Chapter 1

1. The usual cooking and cleaning responsibilities, along with grocery shopping, bill paying, feeding the dog, dropping off clothes at the cleaners, and watering the plants.

2. Changing furnace filters, putting new batteries in the smoke alarms, oil changes for your car, putting in new vacuum cleaner bags, defrosting the freezer, cleaning the oven, filing receipts, scheduling dentist's appointments, pet checkups at the vet, and wiping off the top of the refrigerator a couple times a year.

3. For busy ladies, this list could include any number of items: Church on Sunday, Wednesday night prayer meeting, book clubs, bowling leagues, exercise classes, piano lessons, evening classes, concerts, softball games, ballet lessons, karate lessons, bridge night, golf outings, little league, Boy/Girl Scouts, and Bible studies.

4. Though it is a good thing to be involved in our local churches, we have to figure our time there into our schedules, too! Bible studies, prayer meetings, potluck suppers, fund raisers, vacation Bible school, Awana programs, weekend retreats, church camps, visitation programs, working in the nursery, teaching Sunday school, singing in the choir, being a part of the praise team, missions week celebrations, youth sponsors. The list can go on and on.

5. Birthday parties, Thanksgiving, Christmas, New Year's, Valentine's Day, and the Fourth of July are fun holidays we all know. Some families may also participate in local festivals every year, or go on annual camping trips.

6. Sometimes it's really hard to switch gears from work to home. Being "all-there" for our families means putting away all our work-a-day worries until tomorrow. Children don't know what responsibilities we carry when we're away from them, and for the most part, they don't really care. All they know is that we're there now, and that's just where they want us to be. In the few hours you are together as a family, give them the best of yourself you can!

7. When it comes to important things, many of us would begin our lists with the people who are closest to us. All of us have our niches, though. We have been given a special passion from God for some task—reaching out to the children in our neighborhood, encouraging young mothers, establishing neighborhood Bible studies, helping with the youth group, praying for missionaries. Some women, too, are gifted with a musical voice or a way with words. All of us are uniquely gifted by God, and treasure the way His gifts lend richness to our lives.

8. To use some of the illustrations from the above question as examples— the woman reaching out to neighborhood children might fear alienating their parents. The woman who helps out with the youth group might fear that she's not reaching them, not doing enough. These fears spawn worries, which gnaw away at our confidence in God.

9. "A prayer of one overwhelmed with trouble, pouring out problems before the Lord. Lord, hear my prayer! Listen to my plea! Don't turn away from me in my time of distress. Bend down your ear and answer me quickly when I call to you, for my days disappear like smoke" (Ps. 102:1–3, NLT). Some of my days certainly do seem to disappear like smoke! When David feels overwhelmed and distressed in the face of his problems, he turns to the Lord to pour out his troubles.

10. In the midst of all our activities and responsibilities, we lose sight of the fact that God made us the way we are for a purpose. We are His workmanship—The New Living Translation calls us God's "masterpiece." We are created for good works, and by doing good, we will glorify our Creator.

Chapter 2

1. "You shall not be afraid of the terror by night" (Ps. 91:5, NKJV). "When you lie down, you will not be afraid; yes, you will lie down and your sleep shall be sweet" (Prov. 3:24, NKJV). Still, many of us spend too many hours

of the night tossing and turning instead of getting our rest. When fears come creeping in after dark and wakeful nights come, turn them into sweet hours of prayer, and soon you'll find peace and rest.

2. The Psalmist declares "he is not afraid of receiving bad news; his faith is strong, and he trusts in the Lord" (Ps. 112:7, TEV). Our faith in God, our trust in our Savior, can dispel all our fears.

3. "Don't be afraid of the evil things tpeople say, and don't be upset by their insults" (Is. 51:7, NCV). The New Living Translation calls such insults "people's scorn" and "slanderous talk." Pay no attention to the gossip that is flung about. Don't be afraid of what people might say, so long as you are walking in a way that pleases God.

4. Jesus says, "I say to you, My friends, do not be afraid of those who kill the body" (Luke 12:4, NKJV). And why is that? Because once you are dead, you are beyond their reach. Paul never dreaded death, for he said, "For to me, to live is Christ, and to die is gain" (Phil. 1:21, NKJV).

5. "Do not be afraid; only believe" (Mark 5:36, NKJV). In the face of every possible fear, God asks us to trust Him anyhow. Nothing is impossible for Him (Luke 1:37), and He cares about what happens to you (1 Pet. 5:7).

6. "So don't be afraid. You are worth much more than many sparrows" (Matt. 10:31, NCV). You are precious to God. Don't allow your dread for what might happen overwhelm the truth of God's sovereign love.

7. "God has come to save me. I will trust in Him and not be afraid. The Lord God is my strength and my song; He has become my salvation" (Is. 12:2, NLT). God has saved you—you are His, and safe for all eternity. He gives you the strength you need for this day you are facing. And God will give you a song—joy in the midst of everyday living.

8. "Whenever I am afraid, I will trust in You" (Ps. 56:3, NKJV). We are women after all, and fears do tend to sneak into our hearts from time to time. Whenever that happens, we are to remind ourselves to do just one thing. Trust God! Trust God! Trust God!

9. I love the term of endearment here. "Do not fear, little flock, for it is your Father's good pleasure to give you the kingdom" (Luke 12:32, NKJV). In the face of eternity, all the things of earth do grow strangely dim!

Chapter 3

1. Paul mentions "our fears for today" and "our worries about tomorrow" (Rom. 8:38, NKJV). Fear can prevent us from living our lives because of what might happen, but worry allows that dread to spill over into all our tomorrows. Our worries are spawned by the fears we harbor in our hearts.

2. Solomon says, "worry weighs a person down" (Prov. 12:25, NLT). Psalm 37:8 declares, "Do not fret—it only causes harm." Worry can lead to a bad case of nerves, headaches, stomachaches, and even ulcers. Living in a constant state of apprehension is just not good for us!

3. Everyday worries are common enough. We might worry about making a mistake on the job, forgetting something important, making ends meet, keeping our children safe, getting somewhere on time, being taken seriously, what kinds of friends our kids make, passing the test, finishing well.

4. "Do not worry about tomorrow, for tomorrow will worry about its own things. Sufficient for the day is its own trouble" (Matt. 6:34, NKJV). Every day is full enough. We certainly don't need to borrow trouble from tomorrow. Concentrate on what is before you, rather than allowing the future's responsibilities to overwhelm you.

5. It's not uncommon for new parents to feel suddenly overwhelmed with the realization that they are responsible for a little person for the next couple of decades. They'll start fretting over college educations while junior is still in diapers. How silly! We worry about our health, our weight, our bills, our parents, our vulnerability, our future. And not a bit of the worrying does any good. Plan ahead as best you can, but take your life one day at a time!

6. "Don't worry about anything; instead pray about everything. Tell God what you need, and thank Him for all He has done" (Phil. 4:6, NLT). If you find your mind spinning, and worries consuming your thoughts, pray! Talk to God about the concerns that are nagging at you. Then count your blessings. Remind yourself of how He has taken care of everything in the past. Your worries will slip away.

7. "Give all your worries and cares to God, for He cares about what happens to you" (1 Pet. 5:7, NLT). Even if it is something small, and seemingly insignificant in the face of eternity, God cares about it because He loves you. Give it over into His hands, and He'll take care of it for you.

Chapter 4

1. Depending on personality style, stress affects all of us differently. It can weigh us down so that we're gloomy, despondent, and withdrawn. It can get us all worked up, so that we're flying around trying to do three things at once. Some of us just want to run away. Some of us feel like crying, others like shouting. Many of us find ourselves on an emotional roller coaster, feeling all of the above in close succession.

2. David cries out "My spirit is overwhelmed within me. My heart within me is distressed" (Ps. 143:4, NKJV). Today's English Version puts the same verse this way: "I am ready to give up; I am in deep despair." It doesn't always take much to bring on these feelings. Looming deadlines, noisy carpools, children needing attention, financial burdens, a house in disarray—these can easily become the proverbial straw that breaks the camel's back and plunge us into despair.

3. "All our busy rushing ends in nothing" (Ps. 39:6, NLT). We busy ourselves in vain sometimes, and miss the really important things in life. Our days really are few on this earth, and we need to consider very carefully how we will use them.

4. "A prayer of one overwhelmed with trouble, pouring out problems before the Lord. Lord, hear my prayer! Listen to my plea" (Ps. 102:1, NLT). God is our only help in these circumstances!

5. "See then that you walk circumspectly, not as fools but as wise, redeeming the time" (Eph. 5:15–16, NKJV). Paul urges us to redeem our time. Today's English Version puts it this way: "Make good use of every opportunity that you have." The New Century Version says "Use every chance you have for doing good."

6. Put simply, Paul asks that we make the most of our time on earth. Think of "redeeming the time" as investing your time. Don't fritter it away, or squander it away in idleness. We are asked to manage our time wisely, and use every opportunity that comes our way for God and His glory. Have you been frittering?

7. "As pressure and stress bear down on me, I find joy in your commands" (Ps. 119:143, NLT). Though your day might be packed with tasks, if you carve out some time to spend with the Lord, you will discover a wellspring of peace. Reading His Word will smooth down all the feathers that have gotten ruffled, and prayer quiets the heart.

8. Paul says, "Aspire to lead a quiet life" (1 Thess. 4:11, NKJV). That sounds pretty good to me! We will discuss just what a quiet life *is* in chapter 10: Setting the Pace.

9. "The incorruptible beauty of a gentle and quiet spirit, which is very precious in the sight of God" (1 Pet. 3:4, NKJV). Top off that quiet life with a quiet spirit.

10. "He will not dwell unduly on the days of his life, because God keeps him busy with the joy of his heart" (Eccl. 5:20, NKJV). I'll trade a day filled with stress for one that is made busy by joy anytime!

Chapter 5

1. Are you rushing through your days, dabbling a little here and a little there, but never settling down to finish anything? Do you rush into work in the morning to avoid the mess at home, then rush home in the evening, glad to be rid of your job for another day? If you are always running away from something, you are probably just surviving. One way to describe the difference between really living and just surviving would be the difference between rest and restlessness. Do you have peace?

2. God can use a feeling of restlessness in our spirits to prepare us for something new ahead. If we were content with our lives . . . if there was no restlessness or longing for something different, we would never change or grow.

3. So your crazy life might just be a blessing in disguise. But that doesn't mean you should stay crazy! God is giving you the chance to take a long, careful look at your life. Your crisis becomes a turning point. It's time for a change.

4. Jesus uses the same illustration in Luke's Gospel: "He is like a man building a house, who dug deep and laid the foundation on the rock" (Luke 6:48, NKJV). We are to be like that wise builder, digging deep to ensure a sound basis for our days. Only then will we be unshakeable when the storms and floods beat against us.

5. The New Living Translation puts it this way: "They will be storing up their treasure as a good foundation for the future so that they may take hold of real life" (1 Tim. 6:19). In this case, "real life" is eternal life. The choices we make now will echo on into eternity, so we are urged to build a *good* foundation.

6. "These are the sound, wholesome teachings of the Lord Jesus Christ, and they are the foundation for a godly life" (1 Tim. 6:3, NLT). Getting organized is always a good thing, but don't try to reshape your life without God. Whatever you build on your own strength is bound to fail. Don't neglect your relationship with your Lord. Soak yourself in His "sound, wholesome teachings" and in prayer. He will help you live a transformed life!

7. "Let each one take heed how he builds on it" (1 Cor. 3:10, NKJV). In other words, pay attention to what you are doing! We are all building on the same foundation, but each of us has our own choices to make. God has blessed us with the opportunity to decorate our own lives! Will you build a little A-frame or a cape cod with dormers? Will you have a blue house or a yellow one? Will you have shrubbery or flower beds? It will all be lovely, so long as you choose to glorify God in your efforts. Will you choose wisely?

8. God uses so many things to arrest our attention: the words of a friend or spouse, a comment from a stranger, the actions of our children. He uses the books we read, the radio stations we listen to, the magazine we browse through at the doctor's office. Then there's our pastor's sermon, our Sunday school classes, our Bible study group, and the lives of mature Christians who made it through tough times and shine like gold. Most of all, God uses His Word. The Spirit within us nudges us and prompts us and leads us towards the lessons God has put in our day.

Chapter 6

1. It is a precious friend who understands that you just need to pour out all your feelings so you can let them go. She listens without judging, doesn't condemn you for getting all emotional, and encourages you to leave the frustrations behind now that they've been voiced.

2. Have you ever noticed the funniest comedians tell stories that include embarrassing circumstances, misunderstandings, huge mistakes, and big messes? In the middle of your next frustrating event, try saying to yourself, "This will make a great story!" Laughing over your troubles can take the sting out of them.

3. "A merry heart does good, like medicine" (Prov. 17:22, NKJV). A good chuckle can relieve a whole lot of tension. Do whatever it takes: rent a funny movie, read a joke book, speak in puns, plan a game night. Do something that will lead to giggles. It'll do you good.

4. Proverbs 15:13 is pretty clear, no matter which translation you might like to read. "Happiness makes a person smile" (NCV). "When people are happy, they smile" (TEV). "A glad heart makes a happy face" (NLT). "A joyful heart makes a cheerful face" (NASB). "A merry heart makes a cheerful countenance" (NKJV).

5. "Please listen and answer me, for I am overwhelmed by my troubles" (Ps. 55:2, NLT). When we are feeling overwhelmed, God will listen to us vent. He will listen to what we dare not tell another soul.

6. "Casting all your care upon Him, for He cares for you" (1 Pet. 5:7, NKJV). Though He's heard it all before, and is about to hear it all again, God listens to His children with patience. Why? Because He really cares about us! God loves you, so tell Him about the fears and frustrations that have dampened your day.

7. It never ceases to amaze me how prayer can transform. When we turn to God with a troubled heart, He is able to help us with our tangled emotions. Our anger is defused, our fears are calmed, our confusion is replaced by trust, our broken heart is soothed, and our jealousy is eased away. When our first reaction to frustration and dismay is to turn to God, He meets us and gives us immediate support.

8. "You will call to Me. You will come and pray to Me, and I will answer you" (Jer. 29:12, tev). When we go looking for God, He allows us to find Him. God is listening. He hears our prayers. And, He promises to answer us.

Chapter 7

1. Somehow, it's easier to trust God with our eternal souls than it is to trust Him with the little everyday details of our lives. We tend to let Him handle the "big stuff" and try to cover all the "little stuff" on our own strength. Unfortunately, that can lead to a life of worry and stress. God has told us over and over that He cares about the smallest of details, even the lives of the sparrows and the number of hairs on our head.

2. "It is better to trust in the Lord than to put confidence in man" (Ps. 118:8, NKJV). People are not perfect, and disappointments are inevitable. It is better to place our confidence in God, Who cannot lie.

3. "Those who know the Lord trust Him, because He will not leave those who come to Him" (Ps. 9:10, NCV). God will never forsake His own. We can depend upon Him. He will never betray our trust.

4. All of our experiences have been unique, but most of us would probably agree we have the hardest time trusting God when we can't understand what He's doing. When we depend on our own understanding, we become confused.

5. The answer is either yes or no, ladies, as to whether you trust God to follow through on His promises!

6. If you really believe God, then your life can be transformed by His promises to you. When He says you don't have to fear, you can rejoice and release your fear and trembling. When He says not to worry about tomorrow, you are blessed with the chance to concentrate on the day you are in. When you really believe God's promises will come to pass and live that way, your life will be changed forever.

7. "As for me, how good it is to be near God! I have made the Sovereign Lord my shelter, and I will tell everyone about the wonderful things You do" (Ps. 73:28, NLT). As our relationship with God is strengthened by our trust, and as He fulfills His promises towards us, we have great opportunities to tell others about God's faithfulness. When God is good, don't hesitate to proclaim it. It will encourage your sisters in the faith, and it will draw the interest and attention of those who are still seeking.

8. "You will seek Me and find Me, when you search for Me with all your heart" (Jer. 29:13, NKJV). God is just waiting for us to seek Him out. He wants us to pursue Him. He will lead us right to Him, for He is waiting to be found.

9. "Those who know Your name will put their trust in You; For You, Lord, have not forsaken those who seek You" (Ps. 9:10, NKJV). Whenever we go looking for God, He will be found. He never abandons us, and He never leaves us alone. That is why we are able to trust Him. Like Jesus said, "Seek and you shall find!"

10. "As for God, His way is perfect. The Word of the Lord is proven; He is a shield to all who trust in Him" (2 Sam. 22:31, NKJV).

Chapter 8

1. God has stored up great goodness for you, and protects you from every evil plan.

2. God will be with you in every possible trial of life.

3. If you draw near to God, He will draw near to you.

4. God will touch your heart, and give you a longing to belong to Him.

5. God knows your hopes and your dreams, and He listens to you.

6. We don't have to be strong or perfect. God uses our imperfections and our weaknesses to highlight His grace and power.

7. God is right there with us, holding our hands and promising His help.

8. God is faithful, and will keep His loving promises for a thousand lifetimes.

9. Jesus will keep you strong until the end, so there will be no wrong in you when He returns and brings you home.

10. God gives true peace to those who depend upon Him.

11. God pays attention to our prayers.

12. God will give rest to those who are troubled.

13. We who are believers will enter into and have God's rest.

14. God searches all the earth for people who have given themselves completely to Him, and when He finds them, He makes them strong.

15. God listens to your prayers for help. He pays attention to you!

16. Jesus urges us "Don't let your hearts be troubled." Instead, trust God and Jesus to take care of you.

17. God sees, knows, and will remember all the work you have done for Him. He knows the hopes in your heart, and will reward them in eternity.

18. Give your worries to God, and He won't let you down.

19. Even when you are old, God will take care of you. He will carry you.

20. God cannot lie. He keeps His promises to us, and that is a source of strength to our souls.

21. Jesus is strong, and can help you not to fall. He can give you great joy.

22. Jesus will encourage you and strengthen you in everything you do and say. He has given you a hope that is eternal.

23. What we ask, we will receive. What we seek, we will find. When we knock, the door will open.

24. Though the world may be coming to an end, God's love will never disappear. His promise of peace will be fulfilled.

25. Our blessings are kept in heaven for us, where they cannot be spoiled. God's power protects us until we are brought to heaven as well.

26. The Lord is with you, and He will quiet you with His love.

27. God is with you wherever you go. Take courage.

28. God is a husband to the woman who has no husband.

29. God has given His angels charge over you, to keep you safe.

30. God has promised eternal life to those who put their faith in Him.

Chapter 9

1. Lots of things can go into a reluctance to say no. Some of us are always excited to start something new. Some of us like to be needed. Some don't want to hurt anyone's feelings. Whether we just don't have any good rea-

son to say no, or we're thrilled by some new opportunity, it's easy to get over-extended.

2. "See that you walk circumspectly, not as fools but as wise" (Eph. 5:15, NKJV). *Circumspect* is defined as "heedful of potential consequences" in the dictionary. A circumspect woman is prudent, careful, thoughtful, and observant. She gives consideration to her decisions before making them.

3. "Do not be conformed to this world, but be transformed by the renewing of your mind, that you may prove what is that good and acceptable and perfect will of God" (Rom. 12:2, NKJV). We don't need to try to do all those things that the world says are good. The world's idea of an active, community-minded, well-rounded individual may be *good*, but God's will for His children is *perfect*.

4. "For it is God who works in you, both to will and to do for His good pleasure" (Phil. 2:13, NKJV). God is God, and He does just as He pleases. He loves us more than we can imagine, and His workings in and through our lives are for one main purpose—to bring glory to Himself. When you are faced with a decision, have you ever stopped to ask, "Will this bring glory to God?"

5. "What does the Lord your God require of you? He requires you to fear Him, to live according to His will, to love and worship Him with all your heart and soul" (Deut. 10:12, NLT). This verse makes a good foundation for our decision-making process.

6. Our goals change with every season of life, but Christian women of all ages should be committed to obeying God and doing His will. A woman's role is varied—daughter, wife, mother, sister, friend, homemaker, co-worker, employee, teacher—and God can be glorified in how well we fill our place. If we are spread too thinly, with too many responsibilities, we cannot do any one job well. That's why we need to be focused!

7. Leaving behind the hustle and bustle of a busy world, you could listen to quiet music, get a manicure, read a good book, work a jigsaw puzzle, read through the Gospel of Luke, start a prayer journal, call your grandparents, knit, go for a walk, organize your photographs, paint your bathroom, or go with friends to a movie. The possibilities are endless.

8. "What you ought to say is 'If the Lord wants us to, we will live and do this or that'" (James 4:15, NLT). Make God's will a priority in your decision-making process. Perhaps you can set up a rule for yourself, like waiting one full week before giving your answer to someone's request. Take that time to circumspectly assess your available time, and pray for God's leading.

9. "For you have need of endurance, so that after you have done the will of God, you may receive the promise" (Heb. 10:36, NKJV). Just hang in there, do what you know is right. After all, eternity is just ahead.

Chapter 10

1. When we face our circumstances ruled by the Spirit and not by our emotions, we are unruffled by the unexpected. We don't get "bent out of shape" or speak sharply. We are not plunged into bleakness or terror. Though many around us are desperate and despairing, we grasp tightly to our Hope and remain unshaken in our faith.

2. God didn't promise us an easy lot in this life. We will always be buffeted by some trial or another—that's how we grow. So every one of us has *something* in our lives that pushes us the wrong way. It gets on our nerves, it pushes our buttons, it rankles us, it sets us off, it leaves us feeling defeated. That something could be your teenage daughter, your boss at work, a complaining coworker, your next-door neighbor, your not-quite-housetrained dog, bureaucracy's red tape, your mother-in-law, your finances, or even the ice cube trays that nobody else knows how to refill.

3. Some things in life are simply out of our control. For instance, we cannot really change our husband. Only God can do that. So when he is the source of the turmoil in our soul, we can feel desperate because we can't *fix* the problem. However, we can make changes for ourselves. What do you need to let go of? Is it complaining, criticism, impossible expectations, selfishness, anger, television, late nights, grudges, control, pride, gossip, self-indulgence, unwise friendships, or hate?

4. It is very easy to pass judgment on other people for how they live their lives. Without knowing all the facts in a matter, we decide, "She just doesn't know how to discipline that child. She'll regret that in a few years," or "He can't possibly have a right relationship with God. Look at what he just did." We hang onto first impressions, we jump to conclusions, we make assumptions, and even worse, we pass them off as facts. Even well-intentioned folks can cause hurt feelings, emotional scars, and huge divisions in this way. We are responsible to God for our own lives. We will answer to God for how we have lived. That is enough "business" to tend to without meddling in someone else's.

5. "We hear that there are some who walk among you in a disorderly manner, not working at all, but are busybodies" (2 Thess. 3:11, NKJV). "And besides, they learn to be idle, wandering about from house to house, and not only idle but also gossips and busybodies, saying things which they ought not" (1 Tim. 5:13, NKJV). For some reason, we women have a love for news and private information. It captures our attention and our imagination. Our nosiness allows us to ignore our own lives and speculate about someone else's for a while. Paul says that's a no-no.

6. "With all lowliness and gentleness, with longsuffering, bearing with one another in love, endeavoring to keep the unity of the Spirit in the bond of peace" (Eph. 4:2–3, NKJV). "Bearing with one another, and forgiving one another, if anyone has a complaint against another; even as Christ forgave you, so you also must do" (Col. 3:13, NKJV).

7. In Paul's warnings against busybodies in the church, he mentions they are idle people, who have nothing better to do than wander around from house to house, putting their noses in other people's business. If those ancient women had been busy at home instead, working with their hands and taking care of their own households, they could not have gotten into so much mischief. Are you drawn to the telephone, to e-mail, or to chat rooms? Are you guilty of neglecting your own household when an opportunity to go out comes around?

8. "Each of you has received a gift to use to serve others. Be good servants of God's various gifts of grace" (1 Pet. 4:10, NCV). As Christians, our lives are woven together in the church. We are all a part of the same body. We are called upon to support one another, love one another, and encourage one another. That can all happen without meddling in one another's lives.

9. Hebrews 10:24 encourages us to "Think of ways to encourage one another to outbursts of love and good deeds" (NLT). Get to know your Christian sisters, and then you will be able to show them Christ's love.

10. There are those of us who could be completely happy to stay at home, in our own little world. Our relationship with God is one on one, and we're comfortable with that. Then, there are those of us who couldn't last an hour without contact with our sisters in Christ. We have so much to share, and we live to pray with, encourage, and enjoy one another in the bonds of love. God wants both of these qualities to be evident in our lives. We must strive for a balance.

Chapter 11

1. Sometimes our fears persevere. They seem to keep on coming back, no matter how much we'd rather they stayed where we put them. In the face of those fears, we must persevere in trusting God to take care of us.

2. "Be truly glad! There is wonderful joy ahead, even though it is necessary for you to endure many trials for a while. These trials are only to test your faith, to show that it is strong and pure" (1 Pet. 1:6–7, NLT). The unexpected happens in every life, and we often feel confused, flustered, shaken, and shattered. However, Peter assures us that these many trials are a way of proving that we trust God. The setbacks we deal with in this world are a means of testing our resolve. When we choose to trust God no matter what, He is glorified. And someday, we will receive His promise to us—inexpressible joy.

3. "Count it all joy when you fall into various trials, knowing that the testing of your faith produces patience" (James 1:2–3, NKJV). This side of heaven, nothing will be perfect. We are simply asked to be faithful in the circumstances we find ourselves. These trials are a test of our resolve.

They give us a chance to choose again to follow God. They strengthen our character. They glorify God.

4. There are days when we *do* cry over spilled milk. Little annoyances add up until that last straw—the straw that broke the camel's back—shatters our resolve. Have you ever tried facing your little decisions and actions with the same earnestness and determination a large crisis would require? Don't let the little troubles slip in and cause waves of fear or frustration. Face them bravely, and with grace.

5. "Everyone who is a child of God conquers the world. And this is the victory that conquers the world—our faith. So the one who wins against the world is the person who believes that Jesus is the Son of God" (1 John 5:4–5, NCV). Let the little stuff go. Keep the big picture in view. We have the promise of victory in the end.

6. "If you keep looking steadily into God's perfect law—the law that sets you free—and if you do what it says and don't forget what you heard, then God will bless you for doing it" (James 1:25, NLT). God's Word is a mirror into our hearts. We all know how it is to spend hours in front of a mirror. Have you tried applying that same scrutiny to your spirit? As women, our emotions are our greatest asset as well as our greatest liability. Having an awareness of our own early warning signs can keep us from becoming basket cases. Take an internal inventory of your feelings before reacting to them.

7. "If you are sensible, you will control your temper. When someone wrongs you, it is a great virtue to ignore it" (Prov. 19:11, tev).

8. We have said that God's Word is a mirror for our hearts. It helps us to understand ourselves. It also helps us to know Jesus better. "If you abide in My Word, you are My disciples indeed" (John 8:31, NKJV). Our lives are transformed only when we are abiding in the Scriptures. It may be easy to let your Bible reading slide from day to day, but in doing so you only deprive yourself.

9. "Be sure, then, to keep in your hearts the message you heard from the beginning. If you keep that message, then you will always live in union with the Son and the Father" (1 John 2:24, tev). Stay in God's Word—read it, memorize it, ponder its applications, trust it, depend upon it. We are to abide in Jesus, and we are to abide in His Word.

10. The victory in our lives is not defined by our successfulness, accomplishments, admirers, recognition, answered prayers, or self-confidence. Rather, a victorious life is one that brings glory to God. Be careful of your expectations, for God does not promise us an easy road. Life is hard, and there's no getting around that. But in the midst of our struggles, He has promised to be near to our hearts. He has promised to lift our burdens and carry us through. Things may not be perfect, but we can rest in the knowledge that they are being perfected.

Chapter 12

1. Our Heavenly Father is the God of Peace.

2. Jesus is the Prince of Peace.

3. "In Me you may have peace. In the world you will have tribulation; but be of good cheer, I have overcome the world" (John 16:33, NKJV). Jesus says we will have troubles, but to cheer up. His team will win in the end. Accept His peace in the midst of uncertain times.

4. Sometimes, the peace we feel doesn't make sense. By all rights, we should be restless or fearful, but we rest secure in God's promises instead. Though it isn't logical, it's true.

5. "The peace of God . . . will guard your hearts and minds through Christ Jesus." He is your refuge, your hiding place, your place of safety. He is your peace in the middle of life's confusion.

6. "Let the peace of God rule in your hearts" (Col. 3:15, NKJV). Isn't it amazing? Peace can rule in our hearts—the Bible says so. So, let it.

7. Jesus did purchase peace for us, and so He did pour that out for us. Peter and Paul both urge believers to "seek peace and pursue it" (1 Pet.

3:11, NKJV). This implies that peace must be our aim, our goal. Though Christians have peace with God because of the shed blood of Jesus, we need to actively pursue peace with one another.

8. "Now may the Lord of peace Himself give you peace always in every way. The Lord be with you all" (2 Thess. 3:16, NKJV). Amen!

⚐ ACKNOWLEDGMENTS ⚐

© Clairmont, Patsy; Johnson, Barbara; Meberg, Marilyn; and Swindoll, Luci, *Joy Breaks* (Grand Rapids: Zondervan Publishing House, 1997)

© Clairmont, Patsy; Johnson, Barbara; Meberg, Marilyn; and Swindoll, Luci, *The Joyful Journey* (Grand Rapids: Zondervan Publishing House, 1998)

© Clairmont, Patsy, *The Best Devotions of Patsy Clairmont* (Grand Rapids: Zondervan Publishing House, 2001)

© Johnson, Barbara, *The Best Devotions of Barbara Johnson* (Grand Rapids: Zondervan Publishing House, 2001)

© Meberg, Marilyn, *The Best Devotions of Marilyn Meberg* (Grand Rapids: Zondervan Publishing House, 2001)

© Swindoll, Luci, *The Best Devotions of Luci Swindoll* (Grand Rapids: Zondervan Publishing House, 2001)

© Walsh, Sheila, *The Best Devotions of Sheila Walsh* (Grand Rapids: Zondervan Publishing House, 2001)

© Wells, Thelma, *The Best Devotions of Thelma Wells* (Grand Rapids: Zondervan Publishing House, 2001)

© Women of Faith, Inc., *We Brake for Joy* (Grand Rapids: Zondervan Publishing House, 1997)

CPSIA information can be obtained
at www.ICGtesting.com
Printed in the USA
LVHW031748020720
659497LV00004B/7